PRAISE FOR
ROAD TO AWESOME

From the moment I set foot in Rock Springs High School I knew there was something different about that school. Within a minute I was greeted by the principal Darrin Peppard as he welcomed me as their newest teacher. Again, I immediately knew there was something different about him as a school leader. Reading The Road To Awesome has reminded me of those very feelings and will inspire you in your leadership roles, at whatever level that may be. Darrin was the best principal I have ever worked with, the best school leader I have learned from, and has become one of my best friends. As you read this book you will learn how to inspire others through example, integrity, and genuine relationships. I am forever grateful that Darrin picked up this hitchhiker on the Road to Awesome.

BRADLEE W SKINNER (A.K.A. DJ PHONY STARK)
EDUCATOR | AUTHOR | ENTERTAINER

Road to Awesome is a masterclass of knowledge that provides pivotal concepts for aspiring and current educational leaders looking to improve their abilities and take their schools to awesome.

JONATHAN ALSHEIMER | TEACHER | SPEAKER
AUTHOR OF NEXT LEVEL TEACHING

This journey will steer your compass true North. Be the person you want around you. Darrin's journey allows us to reflect on who we want to be. Only take 'The Road to Awesome' if you want to make the world a better place.

DR. FRANK RUDNESKY | AUTHOR | SPEAKER | EDUCATOR

Darrin Peppard exemplifies what it means to be a leader. His passion to grow other leaders and to get them on their own Road to Awesome is evident in his everyday life and this book. He asks the pertinent questions that make you reflect on your leadership skills and how you can do better for your colleagues, students and school. Darrin reminds us of the importance of telling your school's story and celebrating it. He is always encouraging others to tell their stories, and this is his time to tell his.

MELISSA WRIGHT | TEACHER | KENNEBECASIS VALLEY HIGH

I first met Darrin at a principal's conference in 2016, and when I heard about his school's hashtag, #RoadToAwesome, I was immediately hooked. It was a message that resonated with me like none before. This book is the story of Darrin's journey. Road to Awesome is a book written with heart and energy and written by an educator who has walked the walk. It is truly inspiring and it will reignite the passion of any leader hoping to elevate their game and transform the culture of their school.

DANNY STEELE, ED D
EDUCATOR | AUTHOR | SPEAKER

When you pick up "that" book that changes your entire perspective about education and your purpose, you don't want to put it down. In reading Darrin Peppard's Road to Awesome you will be drawn into this exact experience. Darrin shares his heart, his passion with us in his book. Darrin asks us two questions that helps us put everything into perspective. If it is your first, fifteenth, or twenty-fifth year in education, you will absolutely benefit and grow as an educator after reading Road to Awesome. Personal stories, analogies, and messages from students all combine to create and support the urgent call to reflect, review, and re-ignite your passion for education. I was fortunate to meet Darrin and work alongside him during the 2016 National Principal of the Year symposium. I quickly learned that his passion, humor, and drive were all very real and unwavering. Congratulations to Darrin for making the time to tell his story in hopes that we can all experience that "game changer" moment in our educational careers and then create the change to lead our schools on the Road to Awesome.

TED HUFF, ED.D.
EDUCATIONAL CONSULTANT, EDUCATIONPLUS
ST. LOUIS REGIONAL PROFESSIONAL DEVELOPMENT CENTER
RETIRED MIDDLE SCHOOL PRINCIPAL

The Road to Awesome is not just another '6 Steps' guide to change your school. Darrin instead challenges us to empower those around us to be part of the change process. Are you ready to be that kind of leader?

CHRIS WOODS | EDUCATOR | THE DAILYSTEM GUY

The Road to Awesome is a must read for school leaders whether it's your first day or if you are a 10 year veteran. You will be challenged to explore your "Why" and it will cause you to look inside yourself as a school leader. You will find this book to be a game changer in the world of effective school leadership. There are so many practical applications and strategies that will impact and enhance your schools culture and climate immediately. This book is guaranteed to enhance, challenge, and support you on your Road To Awesome!

RICHARD PARKHOUSE | AUTHOR | MENTOR | ENERGIZER | CONSULTANT
CLIFTON'S STRENGTHS FINDER COACH & TRAINER

Whether you are an aspiring school leader, veteran educator in the field or even a recovering high school principal you will find many nuggets of gold in the book, Road to Awesome. Dr. Peppard weaves powerful personal stories into an inspiring narrative of how to effectively lead shift schools in a positive direction. His unique style of humility and candor gives readers a glimpse into what it takes to be the ultimate game changer that is needed in your organization.

WINSTON Y. SAKURAI, ED.D
2016 NASSP NATIONAL DIGITAL PRINCIPAL OF THE YEAR
2016 HASSA HAWAII STATE PRINCIPAL OF THE YEAR

Road to Awesome is all about the journey to achieve the vision you want to become reality. Darrin shares from the heart a road trip that is possible for every classroom, school or district to grow from good to great to AWESOME!

STEVEN BOLLAR, AKA STAND TALL STEVE
EDUCATIONAL LEADER | SPEAKER | CONSULTANT

Who doesn't like a good road trip? Especially this one, where Darrin takes us on an important journey, one that leads us to developing an awesome school. We all dream of creating an educational institution that offers a positive learning environment for all students ... and the adults who work with them. This is a down-to-earth, genuine man who offers his heart-felt stories and experiences from his years as a teacher and administrator. Hop in and take this ride with him.

TOM CODY | TOP 20 TRAINING
SOCIAL-EMOTIONAL LEARNING AUTHOR & TRAINER

We are all leaders, regardless of title. Awesome leadership begins with an awesome passion, a desire to inspire, and the ability to make those around you better. New and veteran educators alike will find powerful motivation and practical strategies in Peppard's, Road to Awesome. Do yourself a favor and start traveling the road today!

WESTON KIESCHNICK
AUTHOR BOLD SCHOOL AND BREAKING BOLD
ASSOCIATE PARTNER INTL. CENTER FOR LEADERSHIP IN EDUCATION

In Road to Awesome, Darrin Peppard tells his story from the lens of a sitting Superintendent with a myriad of experiences. Spanning a career of more than 25 years in education, Darrin let's us into his heart by sharing personal stories in an honest, thought-provoking way and reminds us through his key concepts what it takes to truly change the game for schools - great people!

JIMMY CASAS, EDUCATOR, AUTHOR, SPEAKER, LEADERSHIP COACH

Authentic. Passionate. Relevant. In The Road to Awesome, Darrin shares the blueprint for building a truly dynamic educational experience on your campus for staffulty, students, and community stakeholders alike. Conversational in tone, every single story lends itself to making your school a better place through tangible and feasible ideas. While Darrin speaks of leading from the balcony throughout this work, the truth is that he has been directly on the front lines of the world of education and he has the positive results to prove it. Having known Darrin for several years now, I can say without hesitation that he is the epitome of a lifelong learner and a true game changer in the field of education. His book will challenge you to think and will provide you with the opportunity to grow, both on a personal level and on a professional level as an educator. No matter where you are on your personal journey with regard to school culture and leadership, Darrin's story will undoubtedly guide you down The Road to Awesome.

DR. PHIL CAMPBELL | JOSTENS RENAISSANCE AMBASSADOR
HOST OF THE GREEN ROOM PODCAST SERIES

The Road to Awesome is a great tool for those who have just started their leadership journey to those who need to be rejuvenated. The ideas are impactful and won't make you feel like you have more on an already full plate. From telling the story of your school to leading from different levels The Road to Awesome has you covered. It is definitely a book I will revisit throughout my administrative career.

JOE SANFELIPPO, PHD, SUPERINTENDENT, AUTHOR

Darrin Peppard has been on the "Road To Awesome" his whole life. From teaching to serving as a principal to now serving as a superintendent, Darrin has lived life to the fullest by investing in others the whole journey. While Darrin definitely gives insights on developing and maintaining a strong school culture, the meat of Darrin's message is in living life to the fullest (an awesome life!) while becoming the best "you" you can be and building on that by investing your time in what matters – people. You will definitely enjoy Darrin's insights and it will challenge you to join him on "The Road To Awesome."

DR. STEVE WOOLF | AUTHOR OF HEART TO HEART TEACHING
SUPERINTENDENT, WOODLAND PARK CO

Road to Awesome will challenge you to take your leadership to the next level. It's packed full of practical, relevant, and implementable strategies that will positively change the culture of your school and leadership. It's time to take your leadership to the next level and this book will challenge your thinking, assess your practice, and inspire you to make real and sustainable positive change in your school and leadership. I was inspired and empowered by Dr. Peppard's words of wisdom for all school leaders, this is a must read for all school leaders.

DR. BILL ZIEGLER
AWARD WINNING PRINCIPAL | AUTHOR | EDUCATIONAL CONSULTANT

Get your motor running and head down the road to awesome with the transformational leader Darrin Peppard! Darrin sets the reader on a course of awesomeness with a proven roadmap to maximize the potential in the ones you serve through your realm of leadership influence. The Road to Awesome gives proven strategies to transform any educational environment supported by stories that brings the message to life! In a world where leadership has never been more important, elevate your leadership skills to new heights with Darrin on the Road to Awesome!

DON EPPS | THE #CHASINGGREATNESS PRINCIPAL

ROAD TO AWESOME

EMPOWER, LEAD, CHANGE THE GAME

DARRIN M. PEPPARD

ROAD TO AWESOME: EMPOWER, LEAD, CHANGE THE GAME

Cover Concept by Angel Castillo

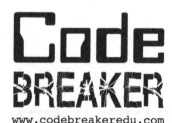

www.codebreakeredu.com

I dedicate this book to the two strongest women in my life, my wife, Jessica and my daughter, Liz.

I love you with all my heart.

ACKNOWLEDGEMENTS

I was certain writing had ended for me when I defended my dissertation. Three years later, here comes Road to Awesome: Empower, Lead, Change the Game. Being honest, it's a culmination of over two years of starts and stops, frustrations, and challenges. This book has not become a reality without a lot of people supporting me, inspiring me, and holding a special place in my life.

I want to thank my mom and dad for their encouragement, support, love, and giving me the greatest model of what parents should be...hard working, loving, and giving of themselves. I love you mom. I love you dad. To Dean and Karla, thank you for the love and support and for having the greatest writing space in the world! My sisters, Christa and Tami, you are the best sisters I could ever ask for. I love you both.

To every student I've encountered during my journey - YOU inspire me.

I've been blessed to work alongside some amazing leaders, teachers, and people who inspire me. I cannot list them all, but some I must acknowledge. To my greatest mentors, Betsy Parker, Mike Lopiccolo, and

Tom Delgado, thank you for believing in me. To those who inspire me, Debbie Petrie-Bullock, Steve Woolf, PC, Michael Wolf, Bethany Hill, and Frank Rudnesky, I thank you for being you and pushing me to be me. To my friends, Bradlee W. Skinner, Eric Lillis, Tom Jassman, Annie Fletcher, Liz Bauer, Jack Daly, Laura Gore, Cori Kassib, Nate Tedjeske, Bruce Metz, Frank Reeves and Ted Schroeder, you've all played an important part in my story and I am forever grateful to you. To Spring Jones, thank you for asking two questions that changed my life. To John Jenson, thank you for helping me get it together. To the greatest office partners ever, Marilyn Rosette, Martha Schake, and Kylee Miller - you are amazing...period. And to my entire #WeAreWestGrand family, I love you and appreciate you all so very much.

And finally, to Brian Aspinall, Daphne McMenemy, and Angel Castillo, thank you for your tireless work making Road To Awesome a reality!

TABLE OF CONTENTS

FOREWORD
BETHANY HILL

A leadership journey is much like a highway. There are moments where the road is flat for miles with not a car in sight, and the air is crystal clear. During those long stretches of road, we can get comfortable and enjoy the surrounding view because we can see what is ahead and predict the terrain. The straight highway has no bumps, no traffic, nothing to slow us down...in fact, this may prompt us to speed up a little. We become confident and in a groove. Life is awesome and getting better every minute! We know where we are headed, and the destination is clear. Comfortability, predictability, and being in the moment makes us feel good, and it is easy. At some point, the road will change. Being prepared for the curves and turns ahead provides a plan for when to slow down, pump the brakes, and turn the wheel. If the driver isn't prepared for the change in terrain, they can lose sight of the road. The road to awesome will have some unknowns, and reminds us to expect the unexpected.

Just as the straight stretches of highway bring us comfortability, we have straight stretches in life's journey where everything is running smoothly and efficiently. Goals are being met, items are being checked off the list, and our leadership is empowering to ourselves and others. What if life was one long stretch of highway? Where would that take us, and would we become better educators and better humans? Think about the times when you have learned important lessons. Was it when things were running like a well oiled machine, or was it during an engine failure with challenging circumstances? When the rubber hits the road, we learn more from the wrong turns, missed exits, and malfunctions. They make us uncomfortable, induce emotion, and force us to think of what went wrong.

The education profession is no straight stretch of highway. Detours will throw us off course, speed bumps will slow us down, and raging storms will stop us completely because we cannot see the road ahead. It is in those unsettled moments that we have to pull over, park, and think about the next action. That could be recalculating our internal GPS and establishing another way to get to where we are headed. It might be exhibiting patience by riding the storm out, waiting and reflecting before the next action. The pause can lead to new routes, or the realization that we are lost and unsure if the destination is the best one. The journey on the Road to Awesome might lead us to a crossroads, where intuition is telling us to go one way, but the planned route tells us to go the other way. Sometimes, our gut tells us the right way to turn and opens up a new view with a clearer vision. The bumps, winding turns, and steep hills are what make us strong enough to be awesome.

Establishing a vision for awesomeness requires planning for a road trip with a team of people who see the same level of excellence, and the leader knows they cannot achieve excellence alone. Expect roadblocks, knowing they are only temporary stops on the Road to Awesome. We will not find perfection on this journey, but we can find excellence if we allow focus and dedication to do the driving.

Road to Awesome places the heart of Darrin Peppard on display. He shares stories of leadership successes and failures that will speak to your mind, your commitment to the profession, and will remind you of your WHY. The Road to Awesome, in my mind, is infinite. We will never officially arrive, but the destinations along the way will leave us hungry to continue driving forward with purpose. That will ensure our vision for excellence is never ending.

So...open the door, take a seat, buckle up, and prepare to take off! The road to awesome awaits you!

Remember to take some time to enjoy the drive.

INTRODUCTION

Allow me to begin with this disclaimer: This book will not change your school. Yes, that's right. This book will not be the game changer!

Having said that however, there are a lot of game changers in this book. It is not the act though, that changes what is happening in your school, district, or organization. It is you. You are the one who can change the game. You are the one who will be the game changer.

I have been an educator for over 25 years. I have had many different roles, from teacher to superintendent. None more life changing than being a high school principal. To this day I consider myself a recovering high school principal.

Yes, you read that correctly. A recovering high school principal. Not that being a principal was a bad thing or that it left me scarred for life. Rather, being a principal was equally challenging and exhausting as it was rewarding.

There are parts of the job that I really miss. Some parts not so much.

I miss the first day of school as a principal. It's different from any other role. Seeing students and teachers on the first day — honestly kids are never more ready to learn and teachers more

DARRIN AND LIZ LEAVING
ROCK SPRINGS HIGH
ONE LAST TIME
2017

ready to teach than on that day! And I got a ringside seat — one I loved so much.

I don't really miss high school dances...I don't think I need to elaborate on why.

I miss graduation. I stood off stage when my students received their diplomas. I wanted to be the first handshake, hug, and congratulations for them when they entered the world as a graduate. I have a lot of great memories from those times.

I don't miss coordinating state testing. You'll learn in this book that I'm not really a fan of state testing, so it shouldn't surprise anyone that I don't miss having to stop learning in its tracks to take a set of standardized tests.

Most of all, I miss time in the halls with my students - I spent most of my time on a bench in the front hallway visiting with kids and staff - it was my office away from the office. It was where I built and cultivated life long relationships that I will always cherish.

There is little doubt that this is a tough time in education. Measures of high stakes accountability may have been in place in our profession for quite some time, but the unintended consequences that followed efforts such as No Child Left Behind continue to linger. One could probably build a substantial argument linking these measures to teacher shortages, challenges with adequate education funding, and the image crisis most schools face daily. I will elaborate more on this, but in essence many schools and districts have fallen prey to chasing test scores rather than what truly matters in education...our kids!

The goal I have for this book is to inject a little energy into how leaders approach their work. To have you step back, step up on the balcony and see what is happening around you for those you're charged with leading. I have written this from a set of core beliefs I hold about school leadership and what honestly matters in the world of education. It's possible you'll agree with me, that you're already doing a lot of what I've written, and that we are kindred spirits. There is also the chance that you'll feel quite differently about leadership than do I. That is ok. We don't have to see eye to eye. I hope that you will find yourself, at the very least, reflecting on your core values and how you use them in your leadership.

This book is written with the belief that we can all do something to make our schools a better place for kids and for the adults who've chosen to dedicate their lives to enriching the future of our communities. If you find one thing in this manuscript that is helpful, inspiring, or even that simply makes you laugh, then it has been worth the time and effort.

CHAPTER
ONE

TWO QUESTIONS

> Two roads diverged in a wood, and I —
> I took the one less traveled by,
> And that has made all the difference.
> ROBERT FROST

Two questions were asked...two. Two questions that are simple in nature, yet have incredible depth.

Two questions that on the surface should be common sense but in reality represent a massive paradigm shift.

Two questions that were asked in a ten second window that changed my game forever...two questions.

My Oma, German for grandmother, was born in Germany, as was my mom, my sister, and myself for that matter. In her early adult years she knew the country long before the concept of East and West Germany came to be. She tells the most fascinating, tear-jerking, and heart-stopping stories about her time during World War II and having to hide from the authorities just to simply survive and make her way, along with some of the family, out of the occupied areas and to freedom. When she tells these stories time stands still and her eyes well up. These are not times that anyone who lived in the area would have been proud of, but they are part of what makes her who she is, even today in her mid-90s. It certainly represents a game changing event and time in my family's history. Listening to Oma and others, who are such great storytellers, may be why I am driven so much by the stories of others. It can be a little difficult for me to tell my own stories simply because I think they tend to pale in comparison to those of others. Nevertheless, I love listening to their stories.

The same can be said for schools. Every school has a story and it continues to be written with every passing day. Some pretty awe-inspiring things are happening. Students have moments of triumph, they're working on meaningful projects in their classes and communities; teachers make new breakthroughs and express amazing creativity. There are extraordinary discoveries and incredible stories everywhere. We just need to look for them!

What does it mean to be a game changer? Dictionary.com tells us this:

game-changer *or game chang·er*
[**geym**-cheyn-jer]

noun

1   *Sports.* an athlete, play, etc., that suddenly changes the outcome of a game or contest.
2   a person or thing that dramatically changes the course, strategy, character, etc., of something:
    Social media has been a real game-changer in the company's marketing efforts.

So, what is a game changer then?

A game changer is an event, activity, person, or moment that, once it occurs, changes everything.

Let's backup a little here. We have all been in situations — work, family, school, competitions — when something happens that drastically alters events from that point on. As an avid sports fan I have hundreds of examples where games, seasons, and even franchises are changed considerably from a single moment or decision.

Consider the long-famous (or infamous if you are a Boston Red Sox fan) sale of Babe Ruth from the Red Sox to their bitter rivals, the New York Yankees. In Ruth's six seasons with the Red Sox he led the team to three World Series titles. Yet, for some reason he was sold to New York. Once arriving in New York, Ruth led the Yankees to four World Series titles. But that isn't where the game changed. The game changed not for the Yankees but rather for the Red Sox. It would be 86 years before the team broke through and won another World Series. This game changer has long since been known as the "Curse of the Bambino".

Another example outside the sports world, would be the relationship turned feud between Microsoft founder Bill Gates and Apple co-founder Steve Jobs. Their early years had them working on projects together, with Microsoft making software for Apple computers. However, a rift occurred between them which drove each to work diligently to get the best of the other. The result changed the game of technology forever.

But what about education? Is there a game changer in our chosen field? Is there a play or a moment that can change the outcome of the lesson, the day, the life of a child? Could there really be a person who can actually change the course, character, or strategy of school? Yes, those people are out there. I've met them. You're probably one of them.

Great people make a great impact in the lives of kids.

Many of them are making that type of impact in their schools today. But what makes them a game changer? It might be due to their belief that school can be so much more for a kid than just something done 'to them'. The truth is that great people make a great impact in the lives of kids. Another truth: you don't have to be an adult to make a game changing impact in your school. You just need a plan and the willingness to do it.

MY ROAD TO AWESOME STORY

I grew up in a normal, middle-class family in central Wyoming. I am the middle child, having both an older and younger sister. I was the kid who hovered in the middle, you know, not super popular but also not an outcast. I had several close friends as I made my way through school and believed I was a typical kid. I was involved at my school, playing different sports, attending games and dances, and even had a girlfriend or two along the way.

I don't believe I had any clear path in my mind regarding what I wanted to do with my life. If you had asked me what I wanted to do with my future, I probably would not have had a quality answer. I learned towards professional tennis, but the reality of it was I wasn't the best player on the team (turns out I wasn't even the best player in my family - that title belongs to my little sister). I knew I would go to college, it was never said out loud but I think it was an expectation my parents had for all three of us. As my senior year of high school was winding down, I was faced with the reality of 'what do I do next?'

The school I attended was fairly large and as such, we were assigned a general staff member as our advisor. Staff members who weren't necessarily equipped with the know how teenagers require to help make decisions about their future. We had guidance counselors, but to be honest, I couldn't have picked them out of a line up at the time.

NOVEMBER 23, 1984

One of my most vivid memories from high school occurred on November 23, 1984. I was a tennis player and a basketball player - player in the loosest sense of the word. I was on the team but that's about the extent of my sports career for any highlights. In fact, I spent more time on the training room floor, table, and slant boards than I ever did in an actual game. I had some pretty tough luck as a high school athlete when it came to injuries. I severely sprained my right ankle multiple times, even landing on crutches for a few of those. I badly sprained my right wrist and had multiple issues with my quadricep muscles. This all added up to quite a bit of time with John Noffsinger, or Trainer John, as he was known to all of the athletes at Kelly Walsh High.

November 23, 1984 was no different. As a sophomore in high school, my season was actually off to a great start. I was slated to be in the starting lineup and was playing better than I ever had before. I was confident and really fit well into Coach Meeboer's offense. This is when that first ankle injury happened. Our final practice before the season opener was a walk-through and should not have been a time for injury. Unfortunately, as I came off a screen, caught the ball and squared up, took the shot (all net) I landed awkwardly on somebody's foot, turning my ankle in the process. This earned my first trip to the training room where I would become a regular guest.

The normal rehab for my ankle injury included before and after practice in the ice bath, on the slant board, and of course taping. It was November 23rd. There were about 10 of us in the training room with the Boston College vs. Miami football game on in the background. It was just another day after practice when it happened. Yes, Doug Flutie had pulled off one of the greatest plays in the history of college football. And I saw it, live on TV, in the training room.

As the realization of picking a career pathway began to settle in, I tried to reflect on my life at the time, all 17 years of it. I had no idea what I wanted to do, yet still knew I would be attending the local community college. As I spent time thinking about what interested me, reflecting on that memory drove me to have an interest in athletic training. What a great life Trainer John had going for himself. He got to be a part of high school athletics, built relationships with students and coaches, and even had a TV in his office. My path was identified. I wanted to be a high school athletic trainer.

I learned quickly that I wasn't as ready for college as I should have been after graduation. Being that my mom was the person overseeing attendance at my high school, I never skipped a class. In fact, I even went to two of my classes on senior ditch day. It was the only way mom would excuse me from my other classes! I struggled in college as a result. I discovered that nobody was checking on you in college and you were free to choose whether or not to actually show up. I was a disaster. Heck, that is a mild way of putting it. I basically flunked out my first semester. I was having fun. And I mean a lot of fun! I was arguably the best pool player on campus. I certainly wasn't putting in any effort to pass a class so I had some time on my hands.

I decided to change my major, twice, to no avail. I even dropped out, got married and decided I would be a working man. It didn't take long to realize that retail sales was not going to be my lifelong fulfilling dream so I decided to go back to college. Mind you, I still had no direction, but my now ex-wife pushed me to get myself together. I genuinely owe KariBeth a debt of gratitude.

Without her pushing me to find something I was passionate about, helping me understand the difference between just having a job versus a vocation, I am not sure where I would have ended up. Shortly after going back to school, the moment I needed came my way. And it was a game changer!

I mentioned earlier that I was a high school athlete. A friend asked me, since I had played basketball, if I would help him coach a team. A 5th grade girls basketball team. I eagerly agreed and found the passion and focus I desperately needed. Within days I had changed my major again, this time to secondary education. The high quantity of science courses I had taken, and the few I'd passed, while majoring in physical therapy were paying off with my concentration areas being Biology and Chemistry. While not everything was perfectly smooth from that point on, including a divorce, I was able to graduate and land my first teaching job in Kingman, Arizona.

Unless your only passion is school, and there's no way it is, you need to be clear to others what it is you're passionate about. Share it with them. I am a huge fan of the Denver Broncos. I can guarantee every one of my students and staff knew that. We should also be working to help others find and pursue their passions. Share your passions and pay close attention to those of your students. Encourage them and help them find their way to the passions they wish to pursue. I spent 11 years as a classroom teacher. The first 5 as a junior high science teacher, the next 6 as a high school science teacher. As you can imagine, I had a number of students in my class for more than one course over their school careers. Sarah was one of those students. She was in my class as an 8th grader and then again in 10th, 11th, and 12th. It was clear early on that Sarah had a passion for science and wanted to take every class she possibly could. Her interests, even in junior high, leaned toward the medical field. We had many conversations over her time as a student about her passions and interests. While I could tell her story, it might be better to see it from her perspective.

STUDENT PERSPECTIVES
SARAH BRADY

Pep was the teacher who wanted to get to know something special about each of his students, learn what motivated them and create a student-teacher relationship that promoted academic excellence. I latched onto his enthusiastic teaching and his high expectations and high accountability attitude. He was the teacher everyone wanted to please, he was quick to praise in public and would discuss any shortcomings in private. This student-teacher relationship resulted in higher grades and engaged students.

I always had a desire to have a career in the medical field. My sophomore year I took the AP

Biology courses that were offered as well as Medical Terminology and decided to go through a school program to obtain my Certified Nursing Assistant (CNA) license. I started working as a CNA 20 hrs a week at a local nursing home and fell in love with patient care. I was disappointed that my high school didn't offer any human science courses such as Anatomy and Physiology. I expressed this to Pep and somehow he made it happen the next year! My junior and senior year he personally taught A & P 1-2. I

SARAH BRADY AFTER
DELIVERY OF A CHILD
IN TANZANIA
2010

loved these courses and had a blast learning these subjects. Looking back on that, this small course addition helped confirm my love of the human body and how it worked and solidified my course in life to become a Registered Nurse.

I did just that at age 21 and remember joking with some of my elderly patients, who didn't think I looked old enough to be their nurse, that I was able to provide narcotic pain medication before I could legally walk into a bar and order a drink. This was a fun way to break the ice with my patients. I have since completed my Bachelors of Science in Nursing and last year completed my Masters in Organizational Leadership. My current title is Director of Intensive Care at my local hospital.

In 2010 I was able to participate in a Non-Profit medical mission organization called Live Now Inc. and travel to Tanzania to provide free health care, assist with surgical procedures, post op care and teaching.

An interesting thing happens when you become a teacher. You spend a great deal of time in college preparing for your first classroom. When you get that first classroom, you realize you have absolutely no idea what you are doing. We want to believe we are fully prepared to start teaching from day 1, but the reality is you can't possibly learn how to teach until you actually start teaching. I arrived in Kingman excited to begin my career and under the leadership of one of the best mentors, leaders, and education heroes I have met in my life. My first principal, Betsy Parker.

As a first year teacher, I wanted my principal to help me grow and be a better teacher and to be patient with me as I found my way. What I actually got from my first principal was far beyond that: I was given a life-long friendship, someone to look up to, someone who would say something that would impact me for the rest of my life. I never considered myself a leader. I was the guy who went with the flow, the guy you SHOULDN'T be following. But Betsy saw something different. Betsy saw me for what I could be, not just what I was. Betsy saw me as a leader. She was the first person to tell me I had leadership skills. I was motivated. Game changer.

TWO QUESTIONS

Two questions were asked...two.

Two questions that are simple in nature, yet have incredible depth.

Two questions that on the surface should be common sense but in reality represent a massive paradigm shift.

Two questions that were asked in a ten second window that changed my game forever...two questions.

After 11 years in the classroom and living more than 13 hours away from home, my family and I decided we would move out of Arizona and back to Wyoming. I was fortunate enough to land an assistant principal position at a really great school in the southwest part of the state. My role would be to oversee all discipline and attendance. I was fired up for sure!

I quickly learned that the staff had expectations of me in my new job. I was to kick butt and take no prisoners.

The staff wanted strict discipline and for students to comply with their orders. I found too, that our leadership team was similar with how we wanted our teachers to behave. Do what you are told, don't complain. I fell right into this culture and before long found I was using the same language used by my peers. The message was clear, let's catch them (meaning everyone) doing things wrong. Punishment will gain compliance, right? No. It won't. In fact, this may be the single WORST leadership strategy you could use. Punishment to gain compliance doesn't work.

A little over halfway through that school year we held a staff meeting to discuss solutions to the two biggest problems in education as we saw it: What are we going to do about hats? and What are we going to do about cell phones? Here we were, spending our valuable time on two things I find ridiculous. When we treat our kids with respect and deliver engaging lessons, they will pay attention to their learning and not their technology as a result. And they'll do so, with or without a hat. Treat your students like you'd want to be treated, with dignity and respect.

We wanted our students to be respectful adults and wanted them engaged with their learning but we were going about this the wrong way. And yet here we sat in another meeting discussing what consequences we could take, or threaten to take, that would make kids put away the technology, take off the hat, and be compliant students between 8am and 3pm.

When you treat kids with dignity and respect, they will often reciprocate.

That's when it happened. I was asked two questions. They hit me like two bolts of lighting.

One of the school social workers, Spring Jones, raised her hand and politely asked, "Why does it always have to be about what they do wrong?" Spring followed up that one with another glass shattering query. "Why can't it be about what they do right?"

The reaction in the room was mixed, some nodding their heads seeming to say, 'yeah, what she said' while others looked as if someone just notified them the IRS was auditing their last 10 years worth of tax returns.

I was speechless.

I'm not sure how it happened but somehow I'd become someone I really didn't like. I look back at it now and realize I was an absolute JERK. I'd become proud of how I could catch kids in the wrong, that I knew where to hide to catch them in the act...it was like a game. It had nothing to do with learning (the whole purpose of school by the way). It had become about me being superior to the kids at my school.

It was Spring's words that changed how I looked at my role. In an instant I found myself wondering why in the world I thought my behavior had been ok. I wish I could apologize to a lot of the kids I punished that year. I knew one thing though, I had a chance to fix it going forward. It was time to change not only the culture and climate of our school but the way we were leading. And I had company. Several of the staff felt the same way - it was time for game changing school leadership, and we would never be the same!

CHAPTER
TWO

CAUTION: ROAD
CONSTRUCTION AHEAD

It is a rough road that leads to the heights of greatness.

LUCIUS SENECA

During my first year as a principal, I was asked to visit some model schools in another state with my superintendent and a few other principals from our district. On the return trip, I sat on the plane with two other people I'd never met before. We've all been in this situation and you know there are two options for the flight. You can put your headphones in, lean against the window, and pretend to be asleep or you can engage in polite conversation with your new friends for the next few hours. I chose option 2. The lady sitting next to me was an inexperienced flyer and was chatty from the time she sat down. She told me about how she was flying for business, was currently an

27

advertising agent for a small software company, and that she had two kids. The third member of our row party was dialled in to some work on his laptop and seemed rather disinterested in the two of us.

At a point, my now long-time acquaintance took a breath and let me talk a little about who I was and what I did for a living. I told her about where I lived (she had no clue people actually lived in Wyoming) and what I did for a living. I'm sure this wasn't her exact reaction but I've seen and heard, well felt, this reaction so many times that it has probably amalgamated itself into one universal move. When I told her I was a high school principal her response was, 'Oh, I'm sorry'.

Ok, wait. You're sorry? Why does being the principal garner your sympathy? I got this all the time. When meeting parents for the first time they would tell me their child's name and follow it up with, 'You probably don't know them. They're a good kid.'

This reaction to meeting the principal, whether your kid is at my school or not, comes from a place of lived experience. Long, old, outdated experience. The truth is, being a school leader is all about knowing your kids and your adults. Too often, parents base their beliefs of what a principal does on when they were in school. In the past two decades, the role of the principal has changed dramatically. The principal is not exclusively the disciplinarian. In today's schools the principal is expected to be an instructional leader, a relationship builder, a cheerleader, a manager, an expert in human resources, a financial planner, a communicator, a therapist (for adults and kids alike), a coach, an evaluator, a custodian, and in some cases a surrogate parent.

If you want to change the game, change how you lead.

Like many new principals, I was not taking my first principalship in a new building but rather one I'd already been working in as an assistant principal. The move from the assistant principal's office I had occupied for some time to the principal's office down the hall was a mere 40 feet. It might as well have been 40 miles. When you switch from one role to the other, it is astounding how big of a change it represents. My predecessor referred to the roles of his three assistant principals as 'sandboxes'. He told us often to try and stay in our own sandbox but if we stray to ensure we clean up any mess we make in someone else's sandbox. He also stressed that our sandboxes were all in his sandbox.

My first official day on the job was July 5, 2011 but I was in the office before that wondering aloud 'what now?' Sure, I had been an assistant principal for 5 years, at this point I was ready, right? NO...no I wasn't (and if anyone reading this says they were ready for their first principalship I'm calling you out). In my interview only a few days earlier I had asked the committee what they wanted from me if I were chosen to lead the school. I believe there were 10 or 12 people on the committee and I can't tell you what any of them said, except for the superintendent. His words were, 'I need you to be the instructional leader of that school.' Ok, great. But that's what I was doing as the assistant principal. So, what did he mean? Was I just to keep doing what I had been? Was I doing it wrong? What else was I supposed to be doing? And what about those sandboxes?

Leadership is never about a title and just because your title changes doesn't mean your style of leadership should.

I spent the better part of July 4th in my new office mapping out what the job descriptions (sandboxes) of the three assistant principals on my team would be and how I would lead their work. Here is where I began to fail...I had the belief that I had to have all the answers. After all, they hired me to do this job, to lead. I better get to it and start leading. Reality was, I had already been leading in the role I was in.

I was only the third principal at that school in 35 years. My predecessor had been principal for 17 years, his predecessor, 18 years. Like most first-time principals, I had a desire to make the job my own, to put my stamp on the building so to speak. In trying so hard not to be the guy before me, I overlooked some really great work he had put in place and a leadership system that was truly effective. It took some time for me to start seeing the errors I was making, but once it began unraveling, they were obvious. I was trying to do it all, to be the smartest person in the room, to have all the answers.

When I was a sophomore in high school, I was a starter on the basketball team and thought I was the center of the universe. In a 5 on 5 tournament in class, I was the point guard, the shooter, the rebounder - I did it all. Apparently I felt the need to demonstrate just how good I was. But my PE teacher had different plans. He taught me a great lesson that day. He slowly took one player off the floor without me realizing. I was a total ball hog! At a point in the game when the other team scored, I stood around waiting for someone to pass the ball in. My entire team was sitting on the sidelines watching me. I couldn't even tell you who was on my team because I had made it all about me.

My first year as a principal was a lot like this. I felt I had to do it all and would get frustrated with my assistants because they weren't doing anything. That was on me. I had gotten so lost in all the 'work' that I had forgotten, or failed to learn just what my role really was. I forgot to lead.

THE MOMENT IT ALL CHANGED

My second year as a principal began with a new superintendent. The previous superintendent had retired and our school board decided the district could move forward best by having someone come from the outside with fresh ideas. Unfortunately, that individual's tenure as superintendent was fairly short-lived, ending rather controversially after 15 bumpy months. It was not all bad, at least from my perspective.

The superintendent came in with many ideas they'd learned from many other districts in their time, and by far their best idea was to provide coaching for all the school and district administrators. Coaching has not always gotten the best reception in the world of education with many teachers and administrators believing coaching is only for those who are the biggest of messes. The reception in my district was not much different, with nearly all administrators feeling slighted or doubted by having a coach assigned to them. I was one of the few who were excited by the idea. I knew I needed some help and welcomed having someone with experience to assist me in my role.

If you were to ask people about the tenure of the superintendent who lasted only 15 months, you probably won't hear anything positive. The reality was that they'd never been a teacher, nor a school administrator. They came into the world of education directly at the district level with a business background. It's easy for people to make assumptions about a person's knowledge and skills based on what they have and have not done in the past. The point here is this, sometimes the best thing a leader can do is acknowledge what they don't know more than what they do.

Sometimes the best thing a leader can do is acknowledge what they don't know.

My leadership coach, Tom, like Betsy, is one of the most important people and mentors I have had in my career. Tom was a middle school principal in Colorado at the time we met. I knew I could be better than good at what I did, that I could be great. But I wasn't living up to my expectations. I felt I was forever breathing through a snorkel with my head well below water. Tom was the model of what a principal should be. He worked with people, trusted his team, and built relationships with his community. I met Tom at his school in Colorado. I spent a little over an hour getting to know him and knew he would be someone that could help me get things back in order. Tom was going to help me be the leader I knew I could be.

Tom came and visited me in the fall of that year and the day was a mess. We met in the parking lot and walked in together. Between the front doors and my office, a fairly short walk, I was stopped by 5 teachers asking for something, had multiple requests for things from students, and my pushpin board hanging outside my office had at least 9 notes pinned to it. A group of parents were waiting to see me, angry about something, and insisted they weren't leaving until I gave them my time. The bell had yet to ring and my day, a Monday by the way, was off to a flying start. This was just another day in the life of my principalship. By 10:30 that morning I had met all the requests of the teachers who needed me, answered most of the notes on the board, and had convinced the parents to meet with one of the assistant principals. Tom and I finally had a minute to talk. I expected we would sit down, drink a cup of coffee, and talk shop. I had no idea what to expect from a coach. But Tom handed me a notebook, a pen, and we left my office. We walked down one of the many hallways at my high school where, at random, he chose a classroom and in we went.

After about 10 minutes in the classroom, Tom stepped into the hallway motioning for me to follow. His question to me was, "What did you see?" I was taken a bit off guard by this. Sure, I do walk through observations and give feedback but he wanted to compare notes. We went to another classroom, then another, and another. Then, we went to lunch. I was missing his point. There are a million things I need to be doing in my office, what are we doing in classrooms? I needed him to help me be a better principal, not teach me how to do walk-throughs. I knew how to do that!

I finally worked up the courage at lunch to ask him when we were going to get to the important work of being a principal. Why was it he thought we needed to go observe my teachers when clearly I had a lot of other things to learn. Tom took a breath, smiled, and said maybe the most profound thing I had heard since becoming the principal, "Darrin, you need to stop being a firefighter and start being a leader and I'm here to help you do that."

It dawned on me when I got home that night that I had not met the requests of my students. How telling.

As a school leader, I had it in my head that my job was to solve everybody's problems. I needed to be the sole owner of information, the smartest person in the room. I had not given any responsibilities to my assistant principals, wasn't using my office manager to anywhere near her capacity, leaving her feeling useless, and was killing myself trying to do it all. Tom taught me, among many things, that a leader is not someone who does it all, but rather a leader is someone who empowers others by trusting them, coaching them, and guiding them.

WHAT DOES IT ALL MEAN?

So, what does it mean to be a school leader? The traditional definition tells us that a school leader is someone who manages the school, is responsible for disciplining students, hiring teachers, and various other tasks. The modern school leader is expected to be the person who knows data, helps improve instruction, and spends all their time in classrooms 'where the action is.'

I was able to work with Tom as my leadership coach for two years. In that time I really felt I had learned so much about shifting from what was on fire to what was really important in the daily life of being the principal. Tom taught me much about leading from the balcony. It is important for leaders to take that walk up onto the balcony and see the whole picture of their school, district, or organization. Great leaders will build systems that are effective, independent of the person leading the system. Great leaders understand that the operational side of their school or district is just as important as the instructional side. Where I had failed early on was believing that being the instructional leader was the work. And being the instructional leader included solving everyone's problems and challenges. During the two years with Tom, I learned how to lead. I learned what really mattered to me as a leader, not just to Tom. Interestingly I learned that I wasn't the only school leader who had these struggles. In fact, nearly every principal will tell you, if they are being honest with themselves, how difficult being the principal is and how very little preparation for the job comes from a masters degree program or classroom instructional experience. The truth is, being a principal is a very hard job and we all struggle with varied parts of the role. I've come to learn that most principals

FIND DARRIN'S DISSERTATION HERE

are not all that prepared for that first job. I was so intrigued by my experience as a self-reported struggling principal and the growth I had working with Tom that I wrote a dissertation on the topic.

This chapter is titled 'Road Construction Ahead' because school leadership is very much a work in progress. There is much we get right about school leadership. Our profession has changed drastically in the past two decades, in both positive and less than desirable ways. Increased opportunities in professional development for educators have given us so many tools which impact student learning. Accountability measures have focused so many educators and pundits to look at test scores as the only metric by which our level of success or failure is based upon. Increased focus on earning academic and athletic scholarships have laser-focused some parents away from the joy of learning and competing to finger pointing and acting the fool as 'victims'. Students are driven by outside forces to be 'successful' by definitions created by people other than themselves and struggle with their own sense of belonging and mental well-being. Pressure to perform is everywhere - on students, teachers, parents, and squarely on the shoulders of the principal. It is my hope that this book will help principals, as well as teachers, parents, students, and others to take a look at their perspective. Go stand on the balcony and think about what is happening in your school community. Is it what you really wanted when you chose this profession? It's time that school leaders take a step back and think about what really matters.

LEADERSHIP PERSPECTIVES
ERIC LILLIS

In reiterating exactly what Darrin said, if you think the job of high school principal is easy, then you are just fooling yourself. With that being said, it is also one of the most fulfilling and rewarding positions in ALL of education. You have a front row seat to some of the most amazing events and instances that you will ever encounter as an educator. A high school principal is not a passenger on the bus, a high school principal is driving the bus.

Now here is the trick. How do you get students, staff, and parents on board that bus with you? That is the million dollar question. I was an "interim " high school principal for two years. I came into the position almost by accident. I had been working in the Office of Curriculum and Instruction, when our executive director called me into her office, shut the door, and said..."I need you to be the principal at the High School, and I need an answer today." Wow!! After I picked myself up off of the floor, I immediately left campus to speak to my wife and then went to speak to my Pastor. Both of which encouraged me to "go for it". I accepted the position, went home that night and immediately began making a list of all of the changes that I wanted to make at the high school. Whoa Eric, easy. You are entering a school with an already strong campus climate and culture, solid teachers, and amazing kids. How hard can this be and how many changes do you really think we need to make?   Time to put a little thought into this before you turn this place upside down, confuse students and anger staffulty with a massive amount of change.

So I stepped back, spent some time in the high school talking to students, staffulty and parents about what THEY would like to see at our high school, then began formulating some ideas for positive change. Leadership is not just about your name on the door (even though I really did have my name on the door), leadership is about listening to those around you, and including your stakeholders in the decision making process. Secondly, I did not want to be the school principal who sat behind the desk, sending emails all day and never having a conversation with, nor ever listening to students and staffulty. I wanted to be visible. I wanted to be in the hallways and in the classrooms forming relationships day after day. Leadership is also about letting others know that you are there. That you are present. That those around you feel like they are seen. And what they do each day, what they are all about, has value. There are SO MANY responsibilities and managerial tasks that a school leader encounters every day. So I just decided to just prioritize. Hear and listen to your staffulty and students, be seen regularly, and develop those positive relationships that are important for any leader to develop. Once those things are done, your stakeholders will get on the bus and ride it with you in any direction, and to any destination.

After this two-year "interim" position as a high school principal, I now have the task of leading a school district as Executive Director. I have the opportunity to lead a very academically-strong set of schools, all of which have outstanding leadership, fantastic students and supportive parents. But also a school district that is stuck in a traditional way of doing things. My philosophy and my priorities will not change, and simply cannot change. I will continue to lead by listening, lead by being seen across campus, and lead by forming relationships across the school district. Establishing relationships and mutual respect and trust with those around you will ease the process of change.

A MODEL FOR SCHOOL LEADERSHIP

I find it interesting how many books have been launched about improving schools and student performance. Books about leadership, instruction, using data, research-based practices, and the like fill my shelves both in my office at work and at home. Some of these are fantastic books and have shifted the landscape of quality student learning. My passion is leadership.

We are in the people business, we can't forget that.

Leadership that is meaningful and impactful not only for student learning but for the betterment of people. We are in the people business, we can't forget that. So if our efforts are simply to improve test scores or the percentages of kids who graduate from high school we are missing the point.

My leadership beliefs are rooted in a passion for bringing positivity and decency back to our society. What drives me to do the work I do, what motivated me to write this book, what makes me want to speak with, coach, and grow leaders of all kinds are these core beliefs:

- Great leaders are crystal clear on their values and align them with the vision and goals of the organization.
- Great leaders know the single most important thing is to continually build positive culture and climate in their school.
- Great leaders know teachers are amazing, hard-working people who lead every day in their schools - and if they aren't valued they will lose them.
- Great leaders know students are leaders, now - not eventually. Right now.
- Great leaders are the narrator of the story, telling not only their stories but the stories of their schools.
- Great leaders know everyone can benefit from coaching, that nobody is perfect and everyone learns

by doing and by making mistakes.

This may appear as a leadership manifesto, and in many ways that's exactly what it is. Traditional models of school leadership where one or few people own the knowledge, direction, and goals of the organization are outdated and do not meet the needs of today's society. If you really want Road to Awesome leadership to happen in your school, you have to be willing to open your circle and give away some of the control. Think about everyone who is impacted by the daily work in your schools. I challenge you to empower your teachers, students, and community members to lead the school with you. In the coming chapters I will push you to uncover what you value, what your vision is for your school, how you will work to ensure continuous improvement, how you will build awesome culture and climate, and how you will tell the story of your school. In each section I will give you steps to build an action plan and will challenge you to get coaching in the process. It is my hope that it will be a game changer for you.

It's time to reimagine school leadership...and change the game.

CHAPTER
THREE

LEADING FROM YOUR VALUES

> Be sure you put your feet in the right place,
> then stand firm.
> ABRAHAM LINCOLN

It was clear a decision would need to be made and it was my job to make that decision. We did not have time to call a special meeting and discuss the necessary steps with the school board. The novel coronavirus (COVID-19) was accelerating throughout the country and had made its way into the state of Colorado. A few school districts had already closed their doors for a few weeks. Our governor hadn't yet decided to shutter schools. The power to make that move was in the hands of superintendents. Making the call to shut our schools down when we had just begun the weeklong spring break could be viewed by some as premature, those without the information made available to myself and to my colleague, Frank Reeves, a fellow superintendent in our county. This decision, in truth, was easy. Easy because we trusted our gut and leaned directly on our values and beliefs.

The ensuing weeks were filled with many more decisions, transitions to online learning, communication to parents and community, support for teachers, and planning for normal end of year events such as graduation. And so many Zoom meetings. It was a difficult time for everyone at varying degrees. And difficult times call for exceptional leadership in order for prosperity and success to happen. Without being political, the entire spectrum of leadership quality was on display at the local, state, and national level. The word 'unprecedented' was spoken an unprecedented number of times. I often heard people say things like, "nowhere in our graduate courses were we taught how to handle a situation like this" or "there is no manual for how to navigate these times." I likely uttered those same two statements as time or two as well. Yet, I will argue there IS a manual for this, you were taught how to lead in unprecedented times. The blueprint may not be written down but we carry it with us at all times. When we are placed in pressure situations we typically will rely upon our gut. That gut reaction comes from your core values. Those innate beliefs you hold sacred. If we lead from this place in times of crisis why would we not then do the same for every leadership opportunity? The answer may surprise you. Often, we allow too many outside forces to influence our leadership thereby clouding our judgement or taking us to places we'd normally not choose to be. The key is being clear about what we believe and remaining true to those beliefs - no matter how difficult that may be.

BEING STRATEGIC ABOUT STRATEGIC PLANNING

Transitioning from being the principal to being a superintendent, especially in a new place, meant learning everything all over again. I had to learn new faces and names, the culture, how things were done in the new system, and what the beliefs and values were for adults, kids, and the community. A place I figured would be a good starting point was the district's mission statement.

I began asking employees of the district what our mission statement was and what it meant to them. Not surprisingly, nobody knew what the mission statement was or where to find it. It wasn't posted in hallways, painted on the walls, or on the cover of student handbooks. It was in policy. Many board members couldn't even recall it being adopted. It had been quite some time since this work had been done. The same was true for vision, it was in policy but nobody knew what it said. The board agreed that we needed to address this and to have a strategic plan in place. The district did not have a strategic plan so my first order of business was clear.

As we began the process of strategic planning, we discovered rather quickly that our community had no interest in strategic planning. Most didn't even want to hear those two words in the same sentence. Several start and stop efforts had been previously made by the board to have a blueprint or plan but unfortunately they hadn't stuck the landing as of yet. As a district, the mantra had been 'Excellence in Education', which was posted and found as part of the district logo. This is even on a banner hanging in the boardroom. This is who we were and wanted to be. So rather than going through the long planning process, we brought our community in and mapped out what we wanted our district to be in 10 years. In essence, we went looking for the values of our community, what was important to them, and what their hopes and dreams were for their children. Years of frustration and incomplete efforts washed away and in time our district had a clear direction to connect with action steps. Three short statements defined our district, community, and the people associated with them:

Excellence in Learning

Excellence in Engagement

Excellence in Leadership

These are the calling cards attached now to everything we do and the lens through which we make decisions. This might seem a bit watered down for those who've been through the massive strategic planning process but the difference for us is everyone knows what we are trying to accomplish. We didn't change a mission statement or touch the vision for that matter. We are clear on where we are, where we're going, and what we have to do to accomplish it.

CLARITY OF VALUES

It is imperative that leaders are clear on their beliefs and values. It's said you've got to stand for something or you'll fall for everything. These are the things you'll stand on the table for, bang your fist on the wall for, and refuse to back away from. I've already shared my core values that drive my leadership, and each of the next six chapters including this one further define them and the stories behind why I hold them close.

- Great leaders are crystal clear on their values and align them with the vision and goals of the organization.
- Great leaders know the single most important thing is to continually build positive culture and climate in their school.

- Great leaders know teachers are amazing, hard-working people who lead every day in their schools - and if they aren't valued they will lose them.
- Great leaders know students are leaders, now - not eventually, right now.
- Great leaders are the narrator of the story, telling not only their stories but the stories of their schools.
- Great leaders know everyone can benefit from coaching, that nobody is perfect and everyone learns by doing and by making mistakes.

There is a common theme in my values. We are in the people business. Focusing on the human being first - their potential, their personal needs, and their value - is the lens I choose to look through as a leader. I have been on the other side of it, having worked with and for others who didn't necessarily lead from this place.

WHAT DID YOU EXPECT?

I was working with a first year teacher discussing her first formal observation. There were a lot of positives yet the level of engagement and student behavior wasn't what I would like to see in a classroom. During the conversation I asked her if the behaviors I had observed met with her expectations of her students. Pure silence. She really didn't know what to say because she hadn't thought about what she expected of her students. I am not saying she was wrong, rather she was unprepared to be in this position without some help and some coaching.

Clarity of what we expect is essential and should match with our values and what we hold important. We have to be clear of what we expect before we can ever hold someone to those expectations. I struggled a little in that situation because I felt I had failed the young teacher by not covering that and getting her clear expectations before the year began. Fortunately for her it was early enough to recover and grow in that area, which she did.

BEING DRIVEN, BEING PASSIONATE

The impact the two questions have had on me as a leader is profound. Up to the moment before Spring Jones fired off those life-changing questions, I was happy to go along with our 'catch them doing it wrong' culture and how I led was quite similar. Yet, every minute after that point I was forced to rethink everything I knew and ultimately questioned not just what I was doing but why I did it. It's so easy to get caught up in negatives and all things wrong in our world. But what's the point of doing something if you're not enjoying it or passionate about it. Too many people go through their lives unhappy in their jobs, their relationships, their choices. The key is coming to grips with the fact that you are where you are because of your choices and being driven to grab and hold on to the things you can control. Then, let go of the things you can't control. This has been one of the hardest but most important lessons I've learned in my life.

To empower people to take ownership of their story and release the leader within.

I am an avid reader of leadership books. One of my favorites is Simon Sinek's Start With Why. In his book, Sinek focused on how leaders and great companies work from why they do something rather than just knowing what they do. I first read this book while in my doctorate program and since have been compelled to keep my why at the forefront of everything I do. It's part of what drives me to be the best leader I can be day after day. I am very passionate about leadership, about seeing leaders grow and succeed, and to see their small victories that propel them to great achievements. It is for this reason that I've defined my why as, "To empower people to take ownership of their story and please the leader within."

Unlike lengthy mission statements that few people know or can remember, knowing your why and really taking ownership of it is quite powerful. Now, it is your turn!

LIVING THE VISION OUT-LOUD

I grew up on a double dead-end street. Yes, my street went absolutely nowhere which made it great to be a kid. We played whatever sport was happening at a given time of year in the street. We didn't have officials, usually didn't have the correct number of players, and certainly didn't have fancy travel uniforms. We just played, and played, and played until we were called in for dinner. Today, specialization seems to be the norm and kids participate in club sports, competition teams, and other activities that take parents all over the country for weekend competitions.

My daughter's experience in school was no different. With Liz as a competitive dance team member, we put thousands of miles on our cars over the better part of 8 years. I didn't mind the dance competitions, they afforded me a lot of time to work on course work and papers for my doctorate degree. Another bonus too many of these weekend ventures was their locations. This provided me an opportunity to venture around the building and see what stories were being told by the school.

YOUR WALLS ARE TALKING
WHAT ARE THEY SAYING?

Walk in the front door of any school, even your own. What do you see? If the building is familiar to you it's possible you don't even notice what is on the walls, the paint, the posters, even the trophies in the cases. But what do people who visit your school see? The walls are talking to them, think about the stories being told, or being missed.

My interest in the look of schools probably goes back to my first year days. When I first arrived in Kingman the school year was still a few weeks off but I couldn't wait to be in my very own classroom. I went to the school and got a quick tour which ended in Room 205. I mentioned earlier I was given my keys but there wasn't much else in that room. Over the next 10 days I proceeded to cover nearly every inch of wall space with posters (movies, athletes, sports teams) showing my students who I was and what I had as interests. Michael Jordan and John Elway dominated the space.

Betsy Parker had one rule when it came to wrapping up the year and checking out for the summer. Your classroom walls better be completely bare, all posters had to come down. This gave our custodial team easy access to the walls for summer cleaning. Some of my fellow teachers didn't like that rule and pushed back every spring. I wasn't in that camp. I loved getting to set the room up each August and always had some new wall swag to share my interests.

When I became a school administrator, I really didn't have the chance to decorate my room. Sure I had an office but that was to be a 'professional space'. I still decorated the office, but not anything like my room was done. The reality is when you are the school leader, the atmosphere and the look of the school is on you. You can be the one to set the tone for how your school's appearance reflects the vision you have for it.

SHIFTING THE LOOK OF SCHOOL

The summer of my first year as the building principal, I was able to really begin shifting how our school was presented. A student, Aly, asked me if she could paint a quote on the wall. At the end of our main hallway was a large display case we had taken over to splash pictures of our students on a rotating television screen. Above the case was just some

DISPLAY CASE QUOTE
PAINTED BY ALY NOVAK
2011

blank (and rather ugly) brown 70's paneling. This was where Aly had decided her quote should be painted. She wrote her quote in orange on painted black panelling, our school colors.

"Someday your life will flash before your eyes. Make sure it's worth watching."

• My Chemical Romance •

Quotes like these became quite popular, with students coming to me frequently with ideas for other quotes along with the location. I had to develop a system to make this fair and equitable, which happened fairly quickly.

MURALS

Quotes quickly evolved into murals. We had a mural project in place for many years in which the senior art students painted a mural to be signed by all graduates at the end of the year. I didn't want that to end, it was and still is an amazing tradition. But I wanted our walls to reflect who our kids and adults were during the time they were there, not just when they were leaving.

Our walls were boring, they told no stories. Nothing about the walls could tell a visitor what was important to us, what we stood for, or what we saw as the vision of our school.

A group of us came together and met at the front door of our school that summer. We decided to walk in together and to discuss what our hallways were telling us. What we found were boring, tan brick walls. The benches at least said that we value our kids as human beings, but not much more than that. Only Aly's quote lived in the front hallway.

ROCK SPRINGS HIGH
2015

We decided that in order to reach all kids, we wanted something that spoke to us seeing our kids as who they were. Not just as students but who they were as people. We wanted to reflect their interests, their values, and for the hallway to be about who our current students are, not just those who came before. We had a plan for the alumni as well.

THE WALL PROJECT

Grace Hopper said, "If it's a good idea, go ahead and do it. It is much easier to apologize than it is to get permission." This was one of those cases. I convinced our maintenance supervisor to have all the bricks in the front hall painted in a variety of colors, giving us a great amount of 'canvas' on which to create. Upwards of 20 - 30 students showed up at various times to put in the effort required to transform the space. The end product was truly remarkable and left

THE WALL PROJECT
2014 - 2015

everyone commenting on 'the walls that speak'. We

THE WALL PROJECT
2014 - 2015

painted a wall with silhouettes to let students know we knew what they loved to do away from school. We are always looking for ways to reinforce good choices. We painted one of my favorite quotes on a wall to keep good choices up front. One of our walls depicts the school crest, now well over 90 years old. The crest was designed by students from the school and still is utilized to this day. This particular painting was done by a teacher and RSHS alumni, Anna Crawford.

IT'S JUST PAINT

Over a period of several years, murals and quotes similar to these continued to show up all over the school. Once our students and teachers had permission to make the school their space, we began seeing more and more of this type of effort. We made our work reflect our values, what we believed in and our vision as a school. Our walls told a story about our students, our staff, and our community. Just

THE WALL PROJECT
2014 - 2015

like with any other initiative or undertaking, without the clear vision or plan, it's just paint.

CHAPTER
FOUR

THE FAST LANE TO AWESOME CULTURE AND CLIMATE

One's destination is never a place, but rather a new way
of seeing things.
HENRY MILLER

When I was in college, I worked as a retail salesman for a well-known department store. My job was to sell hardware, tools, mowers, tractors, and the like. I was fairly good at the job but in all honesty when someone came in needing a new evaporative cooler for their house you didn't have to be a rocket scientist to explain that having cool air when it's really hot is a benefit. There was a period of time where I had changed my major to business, due to my super sharp retail sales ability. This was totally misguided and I felt like a failure at the time. The truth is, I look back now and see the leadership lessons that were provided for me on a daily basis.

I worked for two different department managers during my sales career. The two men, Dan and Jake, were very different. Jake was not overly focused on moving up the ladder while Dan saw management in his future. Working for Jake was always fun and I felt like he truly valued me and considered me a friend, even though I was at least 10 years younger than him. Jake was very good with constructive feedback and wanted to see each member of the sales team improve through support and practice. In times when the sales floor wasn't busy, he would take one or two of us to a product and have us practice our sales work with him playing the role of the customer. He was actually coaching us to be better at what we did.

Dan was not a coach. His leadership style can be summed up by his catch phrase, "Go, Go, Go!" He was driven by numbers and data. He ranked the sales every day by posting each member's sales totals very publicly. I am sure the goal was to motivate those at the bottom to be better but the reality was that sales were driven most by the schedule — the days and times you worked. If you worked evenings during the week, you'd be on the bottom. If you drew Friday through Sunday day shifts, you were an all-star. Dan was only about sales and did nothing, aside from the rank and shame board, to grow his salespeople.

When I left the retail giant to take my first teaching job, I was stunned by how dramatically different my school's leaders were from Dan. Certainly this was a completely separate profession but leadership is leadership right? Working for Betsy was about being part of a team, about being praised for the work being done, and being seen as more than just a body in a classroom. It is amazing what people will do, the lengths they will go when they know they are valued as human beings who are loved and trusted. She knew how best to motivate not only teachers but her students as well. She saw them as individuals, loved and supported them. She was present and visible, and had their backs when things got tough.

It is amazing what people will do, the lengths they will go when they know they are valued as human beings who are loved and trusted.

As a teacher I worked hard in my classroom to make sure every student was heard on a daily basis. I knew that school was a safe place for many of my students. I wanted to create an environment of mutual respect and appreciation. The key to creating this type of culture was knowing my students and allowing them to know me for who I was. Never was the relationship element more important than an early fall day in September of 2001.

If you were alive and old enough to have any memory, you'll never forget September 11, 2001. That particular Tuesday started similar to other days, my wife and I getting ready to go to school (she was the principal's secretary at our high school at the time) and getting our daughter ready for daycare. We didn't turn the tv on that morning and were rushing to make our normal monthly staff meeting. When we got out of the car in the school's parking lot we began to hear the buzz. The twin towers had been targeted by hijacked airplanes.

Our staff was looking to our principal for leadership, guidance, and honestly to hear her say it wasn't real. There were bomb threats coming in about our school and it was decided initially the entire student body would be gathered in our gymnasium. Looking across the room at the daycare kids, and my own child, it hit me that the world would never be the same. For the first time in my life I was scared to be at school.

Later that morning we were allowed to return to our classrooms. I'm sure every teacher in the country did the same thing I did, turn on the tv, watch in awe, and provide comfort for students. Students came and went through the day but a handful of students did not want to go anywhere but my classroom. Years later, we talked about this and they've all said the same thing, 'Pep, I wanted to be in your classroom because you made me feel safe'.

"I wanted to be in your classroom because you made me feel safe."

During my time as a classroom teacher, most of my students worked very hard to be their best. It might have been internal motivation, might have even been from their parents or from some goal they had about their future career. I know, though, that most worked hard because they wanted to please me. This was a reflection of how I worked to please my principal. There was no threat of repercussion if I wasn't working the hardest, rather knowing the appreciation that would come my way motivated me to be the best I could be, and I saw it reflected in my kids.

LEADING WITH A FOCUS ON CULTURE

Leaving the classroom to become an administrator was not an easy decision, nor was moving the family away from our home. There was some excitement and we felt it was a good time, as our daughter Liz was just beginning school. Moving to Wyoming when she was entering 1st grade worked out great for the whole family.

She came home from school one day so excited. It had clearly been a great day for her and she announced, "Mom, Dad! I'm a following student!" My wife Jess and I were totally confused but hey, she was 6. We played along and shared her enthusiasm. We did this for a couple of days. We heard the same thing each night, "Mom, Dad! I'm a following student!" Finally, we had to ask. We asked her teacher 'what is a following student?' She had no idea. I asked the principal 'What is a following student?' Again, crickets...nothing. The following Monday, Jess was talking with Liz's teacher when it hit her what this elusive 'following student' meant. Liz had entered the Young Authors competition and her book, The Big Red Truck, was a winner. When the principal read the winners' names on the PA system she began by saying 'the following students...' So, all Liz was getting from that was her name was called after hearing 'the following students'. She was so excited about this. She didn't know why her name was being called, apparently didn't care either. She was just elated to get recognized over the loudspeaker.

I tell this story often as it's a great example of the power of recognition. The excitement a 6 year old had about something this simple cannot be lost on us as educators. Everyone likes to be recognized. Some don't want the public recognition and prefer to be acknowledged in more personal settings, but the power of being 'seen' and appreciated is crucial.

Back to those two questions, it was clear our school needed to flip the script and stop focusing so much on what people were doing wrong. It was time to start catching them doing the right things! That was going to require us knowing what those things were and how we wanted to recognize them. Lucky for us, a formula already existed and we already had it in our school (and so do you).

WHY ATHLETICS GETS IT RIGHT

You may recall it was athletics that got me into education. I wanted most of all to be a head basketball coach. I was, at best, an average player but had both a love for and a knowledge of the game. During my teaching career I was fortunate enough to be a head coach at the high school level in not one but two different sports. I was a head tennis coach and a head basketball coach during my high school teaching days. I loved coaching, particularly practices. Competing on a daily basis to be better than we were the day before was, to me, the ultimate in teaching and learning. It was easy to measure your progress, to differentiate between athletes of differing skill level, and finding moments to celebrate were frequent. I was reminded of a story by a former player and student recently.

Brian was one of my favorite kids to coach. He was a hard worker but wasn't the kid who was in the starting line up. He was talented but had other players more talented in front of him. He reminded me of a taller version of myself as a player. I coached Brian in both junior high and high school. In the early part of his 8th grade season, our team was playing one of the best teams in the state on the road. We were also considered one of the best teams and this game lived up to the hype. A back and forth game came down to the last minute with the game tied. With four seconds left, the other team hit two free throws to put them up by four points. The game was over — so we thought. Brian was one of the many kids I had who loved to shoot three-point shots so I said, 'Brian, go check in and hit a three'. The play was designed for us to hopefully get fouled and hit a shot but the other team chose not to play defense (a very good strategy when you're up by four). After two passes the ball was in Brian's hands and he drilled the three-point shot. Our bench erupted and mobbed Brian. It was the first three he had hit in a game and we celebrated like we had won. We didn't, we lost...by one. It wasn't the end of the season, it was an awesome game, and our team was thrilled to see one of their own hit that shot.

When Brian retold this story to me, I was reminded why we love sports so much. It's all about competing, being teammates, and celebrating each other when things go right. Brian and his teammates are still friends to this day and I'm sure, along with other stories of athletic success, and probably a lot of stories from off the court, they reflect not on losing a game that day but on how we celebrated Brian.

If you ask about the average American high school, some community members can tell you if the school is 'good' or not but usually can't say much more. When you ask about the football team, basketball team, or wrestling team, you will get a lot more information and passion.

The single most important thing you can do is build positive culture and climate in your school.

Why? Not because sports are more important than academics but because our sports teams have it figured out, and have for a long time. Athletes have the letter jackets, pins, medals, locker signs, and helmet stickers. Yeah, helmet stickers — literally, a sticker for their helmet after making a great play! Think about it. A kid will run through a brick wall to get a sticker on their helmet. The more stickers they have the more 'big plays' or impact they have made on their team. Sports teams have an innate unity to them, heck they have uniforms that kids are proud to wear!

CELEBRATION RALLIES

What would happen if we treated academics with the same type of celebration as we do our athletics? We've all been to a pep rally before. Instead of having one just for our athletic teams at homecoming or before a big game, what if we had a rally to celebrate academic achievement? What if we recognized and rewarded the students who were earning great grades, and not just all A's either, kids who have raised their GPA by .5 or greater? What might it look like if we celebrated grades, attendance, ACT/SAT scores, military appointments and enlistments, and hirings for amazing jobs right out of school the same way my team celebrated Brian hitting a three-pointer? Having done many academic pep rallies I can tell you they surpass anything done just for sports.

A staple at our school was the academic pep rally. The first time doing an academic pep rally you'll find confusion from your kids, and maybe your adults as well. But schools were built for learning, not for football.

GIVE IT A THEME

Having a theme to your rallies will bring even more energy to the event. The decision we'd made was to have our first academic rally of the year at Halloween. It fell right at the end of the first quarter and I convinced the principal (I was still AP at the time) to let the students wear their costumes that day. The kids BROUGHT IT and had so much fun. Yes, fun — school can and should be fun. Many of our staffulty even came in costumes. This became one of the most anticipated events of the year. A few of the themes we've used have been:

- Superheros
- Price is Right
- Halloween Horror Movies
- Mission Possible
- The Tonight Show w/Jimmy Fallon
- Super Villains
- ZombieLand

GAMES

Kids are great at this. Create games that kids can play and compete against each other. Keep score by grade level. Everyone wants to beat the seniors, and they almost never do!

SPOTLIGHT

Put all the students who have hit the targets you've set under the spotlight. Call out or bring to the floor your 4.0's, 3.5's, even better bring out the kids who've raised their GPA by .5 or more. They never get the spotlight — make a big deal of them, they deserve it! Get staffulty involved with a teacher flash mob, a dance-off vs. students, or a lip sync contest. And candy, have candy to throw. Make t-shirts with the theme and throw those into the crowd. Crank the music, sing along, have your drumline perform. Blow the roof off the building!

Bring the games, bring the themes, and celebrate all the awesome work your students and your staffulty are doing every day.

GRILLS, GREATNESS, AND MORE

At our high school, we called our positive referral cards the 'Road to Awesome' cards. Anyone could nominate anyone else for the Road to Awesome (RTA), they just needed to fill out the form. It might be a teacher nominating a student for doing well on a test, for helping another student, or for just being caught doing it right. Once the forms were in, we had a monthly deadline, all RTA card recipients were given a little ticket stub the day before the event.

On the day of the event, the ticket holders came outside by the cafeteria during their lunch and were treated to a full-scale barbeque feast. Hamburgers, hot dogs, beans and potato salad, chips and sodas and water. I would partner up with a few other staffulty to man the grills. This is a fun opportunity to do something a little different and to just 'be' with kids and staffulty. A quick variation on this topic,

DARRIN & ASSISTANT
PRINCIPAL SCOTT WINTER
2016

when the temperature starts to drop, bring the action inside. Chilli nachos, hot dogs, or even a sandwich bar is an option to still feed and recognize while the grill stays out of the snow.

MAD PROPS MONDAY

Keeping with the concept of recognizing, rewarding, and reinforcing the right behaviors, the awesome kids of West Grand High School developed 'Mad Props Monday'. Similar to the Road To Awesome cards, this variation of catching them doing it right gives everyone

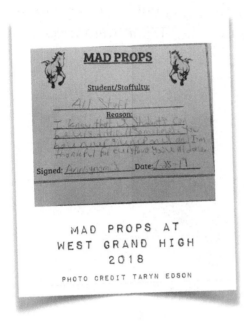

MAD PROPS AT
WEST GRAND HIGH
2018

PHOTO CREDIT TARYN EDSON

in the school community the opportunity to give a shout out to those who are doing it right. Every Monday during the announcements, the students read all the Mad Props over the PA system, giving the shout out they deserve.

Giving our kids that "I'm a following student" feeling was something we were very proud of. We were creating a culture of positivity and belonging. We were building relationships and making connections.

TRAVELLING TROPHIES

Traveling trophies allow staffulty members to recognize their peers in a public fashion. It's simple, pick any traveling trophy — a golden apple, horseshoes, a bowling pin, anything — and present it to the first recipient in a staffulty meeting or another public gathering. From there, the staffulty who receive the trophies must bring them back to the next meeting and recognize one of their peers.

My favorite version of the travelling trophy belonged to West Grand K8. Our schools are the Mustangs, Colts, and Buckaroos. The K8 decided their traveling trophy would be an actual horseshoe on a massive gold chain. If you are a college football fan, think University of Miami's turnover chain. It was a huge hit!

GETTING CUSTODIANS INVOLVED

Similar to the travelling trophy, this award is a must for elementary school classrooms. Kids are competitive, and so are their teachers. The concept here is to work with your custodians and have them select weekly the cleanest classroom. Students will work very hard to make sure they are cleaning up after themselves and this gives the custodian connection to the

LIBRARY TRAVELING TROPHY
WEST GRAND ELEMENTARY
2019

work being done on culture and climate. The cleanest classroom gets to have the golden trash can for one week. It then rotates to the next winner. Other variations of this traveling trophy can be tied to student behavior, cooperation, quiet transitions in the hallway or other areas of focus.

This is where you have an opportunity to capitalize on the people in your community who want to help out but aren't necessarily available to come into your school. At West Grand K8, the traveling trophies for music, PE, and library were made by the spouse of a teacher. His fabrication skills are incredible.

No program, curriculum, or initiative will reach is peak benefit without a culture and climate where everyone feels valued and part of something special.

GIVE THEM SPACE

Early in my administrative years, I noticed that our students were sitting on the floor of the hallways because there were no other options for them. Fortunately we had our gymnasium remodelled that summer and had an enormous amount of wood planks from the old bleachers left over. In a conversation with a few of the maintenance technicians they brought up the idea of making benches out of the old wood. Within the span of just a year, we had benches lining nearly every open space in our hallways. They looked great and served a much needed function. Even better, they cost next to nothing since we had most of the supplies.

RSHS LEADERSHIP TEAM 2015

L-R DARRIN PEPPARD, ANNIE FLETCHER, THOMAS JASSMAN, CLAY JARVIE (SRO), BRADLEE W. SKINNER

Our students were very appreciative but some of the teachers were a bit skeptical. 'What if they vandalize them?' they would say. 'What if they don't' was my response. It turned out we had very little if any damage done to the benches. In fact they still remain in excellent condition.

PRIDE IN YOUR SCHOOL

To start with, clean it up! This may not seem worthy of being a game changing element in your school's culture and climate, but if you don't have enough pride to keep it looking great why would anyone else take pride in your building? Early on in my administrative career, I would walk the halls at lunch, patrolling the campus to ensure mischief wasn't a foot. We had a rule, among the many rules, that food wasn't allowed outside of the cafeteria. This was problematic to say the least. At the time we had well over 1,000 students and a cafeteria with a capacity of 260. Using three lunches for the campus helped, but expecting our kids not to have food or drinks in our hallways was unrealistic. The most common issue was trash being left on the ground in many parts of the campus. We were taking the same approach that many schools still use to this day, 'if they can't take care of their trash, let's outlaw food and drink!'

We were looking at the issue all wrong and were trying to fix the symptom rather than treat the root cause. Kids are not messy on purpose, really they aren't. (ok, maybe a few but not all of them) In fact, the vast majority of kids will do the right thing and make good choices when presented with the option. So, how do you give them the right options? Treat the root cause, Disney style.

Millions of people visit the Disney parks every year. Somehow with that high volume of patrons the parks are amazingly well maintained and extremely clean. In the early years of the original park's opening, Walt Disney became obsessed with ensuring the park would remain in pristine condition. In a rather casual study, Walt noticed the average patron would hang on to their garbage no further than 30 feet. It is no coincidence that even today the park is meticulous about having trash receptacles equally spaced throughout. And you will find very little, if any, trash. My school took on this same approach, adding trash cans at roughly the same distance. The result was amazing. We didn't have to ban their beverages or snacks, just simply give them a place for their garbage. They weren't perfect but it was so much better and the building's appearance improved dramatically.

CREATING CULTURE BUILDS CONNECTIONS

The first day of our winter break the year Aly painted that first quote was a Friday. Aside from a few custodians and a couple of the secretaries, I had the building to myself. The beginning of a break is always a time to decompress and to just breathe, at least for me. This year was no exception. I've said it before but being a first year building principal is HARD work and I was exhausted.

Somewhere in the middle part of the morning one of my secretaries came in and, through eyes filled with tears, shared tragic news. That morning, Aly had died in a single car accident and another of our students was hurt pretty badly in the wreck. I was devastated, in complete shock. I found myself standing not long after the news came beneath Aly's quote.

"Someday your life will flash before your eyes. Make sure it's worth watching."

• My Chemical Romance •

Before I knew it, a few students had made their way into the school and joined me in that front hallway. The further into the day we went, the more students and staffulty began to show up. By dinner time, the hall was filled and a vigil planned for the space right outside the door. I knew it was important that day for me to be there with my students, my staffulty. But it was hard, I was grieving and in shock. My heart was broken for her family and for our school community.

It was a common space for me, that hallway was really my true office. But sitting on a bench that day was both awful and unifying. Tragedy has a way of bringing people together. I was given an amazing insight into the mind of our students that day. A young man, Chase, who was one of the best student leaders I'd ever had, sat with me quite a bit that day. He was one of the first kids who showed up at the school in the morning. As the evening began to get quiet and people returned to their homes, Chase put his arm around me and said, 'Pep, how are you doing?' Through the tears I said, 'Chase, I'm crushed but I am glad I could be here for all of you.' I will never forget what he said in response,

'Pep, we all love you and appreciate that, but you should know I wanted to be here for you.'

The culture we created in our building helped build the connections we experienced that day — connections that leave life-long lasting impressions.

THIS CHAPTER IS DEDICATED TO THE MEMORY OF ALY NOVAK

CHAPTER
FIVE

NAVIGATING THE ROAD TO AWESOME WITH STAFFULTY

> Teachers have three loves: love of learning, love of learners, and the love of bringing the first two loves together.
> SCOTT HAYDEN

I recently had a conversation with a good friend who was moving from his role as a building principal into a new role at the district level. He is now serving as an assistant superintendent in a different community. In addition to learning a new community, new building, new relationships, and navigating a new system, he was faced with the dilemma of working in a role that placed him as a liaison between the superintendent and a group of principals.

During our conversation he asked me for some advice. How do we move from being a building principal to being someone who now is supposed to lead a group of principals? How do I help these unique individuals lead their schools, each of which has its own challenges and strengths, while also meeting the goals and directives of my superintendent? This was such an interesting line of questioning. I have been able to build quite a good network of leaders from all over the country, but none that had impressed me more as a true servant leader than this man. My answer to his questions came in the form of a question.

Who is it you really serve?

As leaders, it is essential we do not forget to revisit this question often. Who do we really serve and how do we best do it? It might be the quick and easy answer to say we serve our students. This would be an accurate assessment. However, I ask leaders to think a little deeper about this question. If we want to grow our kids, to serve our kids, as leaders the conduit through which we impact kids is our teachers. In fact, if you want to grow and serve your students as a leader the most important thing you can do is grow and support your teachers. So again, who is it you really serve?

SOME DISTURBING TRENDS

Research shows that teachers, especially those early in their careers, are leaving the profession at a rather high rate. The reasons many cite for career changes are:

- Challenging Work Conditions
- Feeling Unnoticed & Disrespected
- Testing & Data
- Emotional Exhaustion & Burnout
- Pay vs Performance

Think about these five primary reasons for teachers leaving our profession. I am drawn to the realization that we, as leaders, have a great deal of control over many of these issues. While I realize we aren't all legislators or employees of state departments of education, we can and do have a say in the work conditions our teachers are facing. It comes back to the question above, who is it that you really serve?

There is no doubt that we serve our students. The question we need to reflect on is how we are serving them. We are not the people in the classroom every day. We are not the ones creating lessons, looking at individual student data, losing sleep over the home life a student is faced with every night. We may care deeply about our students but we are not their teacher. We aren't the paraprofessionals in the class each day assisting a student with special needs, changing a diaper or feeding tube. So I will ask again, who is it that you really serve? My answer would be that you serve your staff.

STAFFULTY (STAFF + FACULTY)

I approach this a little differently than most and, again, I am a culture builder so I'm passionate about the importance of everyone, not just the teachers. Earlier I wrote that no program, curriculum, or initiative will reach its peak benefit without a culture and climate where everyone feels valued and part of something special. I've also stated we are in the people business and we can't forget that, ever! I place an equal value on every person working with kids in my schools. Saying staff and faculty can be somewhat divisive. It creates a hierarchy and implies that the teachers are much more important than a paraprofessional, librarian, bus driver, food service worker, or custodian. A core belief I hold is that we are all in this together. We therefore must act like we are all in it together. The person who impacted me the most as a student was the high school athletic trainer. Was he any less important than my English or Science teacher? Not in my eyes, not in my eyes.

GIVING ROOM TO INNOVATE

As a first year teacher I was given keys and a room number. Not much else. It was my job to figure out what was important for students to learn in 8th grade science. We had a basic curriculum outline, but Betsy believed in letting her teachers work to their strengths, collaborate, and focus on growing the whole child. I was a rookie teacher at the time the No Child Left Behind Act had passed. Most legislatures, state departments of education, and district leaders were still not sure what this legislation would mean, let alone a first year teacher. What I learned is that every child is so much more than just a set of test scores. It is for that reason I look for teachers who are willing to innovate in their classrooms rather than simply teach to a test.

Teachers today have so many expectations on their plates. Meeting state standards can be very challenging for even the very best teachers. We expect our teachers to have and hold high expectations of their students and to deliver engaging lessons on a daily basis. When leaders follow their core beliefs they convey a clear and consistent message to teachers. Trusting them to bring skills they have mastered into their classrooms is one of the finest compliments leaders can pay their teachers. I consider compliance to be the enemy of innovation. When teachers are given the freedom to innovate and to take risks in their classrooms without fear of reprisal, amazing things happen.

Compliance is the enemy of innovation.

How do busy school leaders best support teachers and staffulty who are trying to be innovative in their teaching practice? You "Give them Five"!

- Give them Your Ear
- Give them Space
- Give them Time
- Give them Coaching
- Give them Praise

GIVE THEM YOUR EAR

I have been the one who will just jump into something and be comfortable with building it on the fly. Not everyone is wired this way and might need a sounding board. Quite often, we believe that leading means having the solutions to every problem that might be brought our way. As a school leader, staffulty will come to you frequently with areas of struggle or ideas they might be considering. Instead of rushing to being the one with the answers try asking this question first: What do you want to do?

I learned this strategy when working as a principal and having assistant principals who were new to the role. It's easy to tell them the answer or what they should do. However, when asked, they will pause and think and most likely come to a similar or better solution than what you had in mind.

When teachers are struggling with something or have an idea that might be different from their regular practice one of the most effective strategies is to hear them out. I know I'm often in need of a sounding board, why would it be any different for our teachers, our librarians, or our custodians? Listening can quickly be overlooked as a communication skill but there may not be a more important tool for leaders. We must be sure we are always listening to understand rather than listening simply to respond.

GIVE THEM SPACE

I broke a bone in my right hand when I was in the 7th grade. My hand was in a cast for a little over six weeks and, being right-handed, everything became a challenge for me. I tried to write with the cast but it proved too difficult. I chose to learn to write left-handed. Anyone who has encountered this or something similar knows how change can be rather frustrating. The same holds true for anyone trying something new in their classroom or job role. Just like my teachers allowed me the opportunity to test out my left-handed experiment, give your innovators the luxury of space. Let them know you support their efforts and are available to them when they need you, but don't smother those who are trying something creative or a variance from the norm. When given space, you will notice your teachers willingly keeping you updated on their efforts and new learning.

GIVE THEM TIME

Research shows the number of repetitions necessary to master a new skill could range between 1,000 and 3,000 reps. This is true for learning to make a layup, hit a forehand on the tennis court, or hitting a golf ball. It makes sense then to carry this forward to learning a new skill or strategy in a classroom. Teachers need time when they are working on new material and moves in the classroom. Expecting change to happen quickly or to be manifested in any form of data while still learning to perfect technique is unrealistic. Patience is one of the best forms of support you can provide to any staffulty working to improve.

GIVE THEM COACHING

When anyone is working to improve their skill set, having another set of eyes and some honest feedback will make a tremendous impact. Coaching can often be viewed as only for teachers needing an 'improvement plan'. Nothing could be further from the truth. When I was learning to write with my left hand I would watch the left handed students in my classes. I would pay attention to how they held their pencil, positioned their arm, and how they moved their wrist. It looked dissimilar to how I created the motion of writing with my right hand. I tried to replicate their movements and eventually my penmanship and speed improved. Now, having a coach for ambidextrous undertakings might be a bit out there, but I've heard similar things when talking about coaching teachers. Being there for teachers when they are working through a new skill to give feedback and to coach them through the process is essential. Sometimes as a coach you will model, sometimes you will be a cheerleader. Either way, coaching is important in the process of continual improvement.

GIVE THEM PRAISE

For any innovative practice to happen in schools, leaders must demonstrate the willingness to support the work. When our adults are working hard to try things that are things that are innovative or out of their comfort zone, they are showing a lot of bravery and vulnerability. For that reason, it is critical they are praised for their efforts. Do not simply praise successful endeavors, rather shine spotlights on those who tried and are making adjustments to their new practices. When educators know they have the chance to try things that can improve performance of their students, things that reinvigorate and bring excitement to schools, they will continually strive for more.

The opposite holds true in an environment where teachers are afraid of punishment and/or consequences. They will not try new things and innovation will not happen. It takes a great deal of effort to build a culture where teachers feel secure and comfortable taking risks. In a time in education when many are chasing test scores and working toward uniformity in classrooms, placing trust in staffulty to be creative and to innovate within their own space is a big game changer!

GROWING STAFFULTY

In order to best grow our students leaders must grow the adults working closest with them. Leaders push every day for teachers to differentiate their lessons, to meet their kids where they are, and to help raise every kid to a standard. Teachers cannot be successful using a one-size-fits-all approach. We would never advocate for a teacher to 'teach to the middle' and be ok with the results. Why would leaders then use the same approach to professional learning for teachers?

Think of it another way. My doctor sees about 40 patients every day. Each patient comes in for a different ailment or reason that requires his skills and services. If a doctor were to use the same diagnosis and treatment plan for every patient seen in a given day they'd probably be sued for medical malpractice. Could the same be said for professional development for teachers?

If we ask every teacher to do the exact same thing and prescribe identical strategies regardless of the content, age group, or ability of their students we could be guilty of educational malpractice.

Instead, consider growing teachers in a fashion similar to what should be asked of them in the classroom. Personalizing professional development allows teachers to select growth opportunities applicable to their own work and to the needs of their students. Early returns on this practice have shown greater teacher engagement in professional learning as well as increased implementation of practices and strategies teachers learn. Don't make professional learning only for strategies either. Give staffulty the opportunity to select time to plan and implement into their lesson plans, give time for self-care like yoga, blogging, reading, walking, and meditation. Having a work environment focused on learning is crucial, but making the environment focused on the actual needs of the adults doing the learning models and mirrors what should be asked in classroom practice.

STAFFULTY LOVE

Leading a school can drive a person to focus simply on the work at hand. Ensuring the right curriculum, resources, and supplies are in the hands of educators is important. Building relationships with parents and continually balancing the partnership with them that is so essential to student success takes up a lot of a leader's time. Being available and visible at events and present in the halls to support students shows how much a leader cares and that they 'get it'. But making an impact on those closest to the kids, the staffulty, is the essence of leading a school. I have been asked often what I think the most important thing leaders can do to impact their staffulty is. I think the answer is simple. You have to love them. Just like with kids, if they know how much you care about them they are willing to do nearly anything on your behalf. The most important thing staffulty can do for me is live the vision we have for our district and our schools. I have no doubt that because they know I love them they will live that vision out loud.

For clarity, don't go running around telling your staff 'I love you' just because you read this book. That is not the point. You can show them through your actions.

STARFISH FOR INSPIRATION

As the story goes, a little girl is on the beach throwing starfish back into the ocean after high tide. A man running by stopped and asked, 'what are you doing?' The girl responds by explaining she is throwing the starfish back into the ocean because if she doesn't they will die. The man, noticing the beach being littered by starfish, says 'you can't possibly make a difference, there are too many.' The girl, picking one up and throwing it back says, 'I made a difference for that one.'

Every day we are given the opportunity to make a difference in the lives of others. They, too, make a difference for us. It is for this reason that I wear a starfish pin every day. I purchase little bookmarks that have the starfish story on them. The bookmarks also have two starfish pins attached. The idea is to give a bookmark to someone who has made a difference for you. They keep one pin and then hand the other one off to someone who has made a difference in their life.

I have been giving starfish pins away for quite some time. I enjoy seeing the response of others and hearing their stories about people who have inspired them to action. As an example, Jennifer Stuart (2019 West Grand Teacher of the Year) shared this story with me about the power of paying the starfish forward after receiving a starfish of her own.

PAYING IT FORWARD
JENNIFER STUART

Jaime Franklin, a teacher at WGSD, grew up in Grand County. She was given the starfish award. The teacher that inspired and impacted her, Tami Cherrington, has since retired, but Jaime kept the second starfish in her car in hopes that she would encounter her. She was out to eat one night when she spotted this special teacher out to eat with her husband at the same restaurant. She quickly went to her car to retrieve the starfish and approached their table. Tami immediately recognized her and they shared in a joyful reunion. Fighting back tears, Jaime took out the starfish and told Tami that she had been granted the starfish award for inspiring and caring so much about her students. She went on to say that when she was granted this honorary award, she was given a second starfish to give to the person who inspired and impacted her life.

JAIME (LEFT)
AND TAMI
(RIGHT)

She then presented the retired teacher her second starfish. She told her that it was for the lessons she taught that extended far beyond the classroom walls. She thanked her for her unconditional love, support, and positive influence. They hugged and Tami thanked her. Through the starfish award, Jaime was able to recognize that one teacher that she felt so fortunate to have in her educational journey, and for that, she is extremely grateful.

HANDWRITTEN NOTES

I have mentioned already what a huge impact Betsy, my first principal, has had on my life. This game changer is no different. Many different variations of handwritten notes can be created, but this story begins during my second year in teaching.

My grandpa was an a m a z i n g woodworker. My house was filled as a kid with lamps, boxes, tables, coin containers. If you could make it out of

HAND WRITTEN NOTE
FROM BETSY PARKER
1996

wood, chances were we had it at our house and it was made by my grandpa in his shop in Afton, WY. I still have many of his creations in my possession but the one I've always treasured the most is a small box with my name inside the lid. It is a beautiful box and, upon getting my very own classroom, I couldn't wait to have it on my desk. I've kept a variety of things in the box throughout my lifetime, but after finding a handwritten note on a post-it from my principal, nothing else has been allowed to share that space. This note from 25 years earlier still means the world to me. It is STILL in the box on my office desk at home!

Over the course of my career as a leader, I have been very intentional about my handwritten notes. Often when I have something we give to staffulty, I will put it in the classroom, workspace, or on their desk with a handwritten note. One year I did coffee tumblers for everyone and put them in their spaces with a note. Another year, lapel pins stating 'I Love My School' again with handwritten notes. The list goes on but there is one constant. The item may or may not stay in their possession but I find those handwritten notes taped to their filing cabinet, on their board held up with magnets, or slid behind the plastic of a notebook they use daily. Another simple twist on this is birthday cards. It's one thing to get a birthday card from your boss, but when that card has a personal note and their signature, it means a lot more. Just like with my note all those years ago, the handwritten note conveys how much you genuinely care much more than any item you might purchase.

CAFETERIA TAKEOVER

Schools are so good at putting together luncheons and potluck meals. If there is an event to celebrate, we bring the food. These are such great ways to get our staffulty together but they tend to happen over the lunchtime hour. As a result, the group that gets left out are the amazing folks in nutrition services/food service or whatever term you are using for the cafeteria staff. Here is a great little game changer to give them the recognition they deserve and to honor their work.

WEST GRAND LEADERS TAKE OVER THE CAFETERIA 2018

L - R DOMINIQUE JONES, DARRIN PEPPARD, LIZ BAUER, MARTHA SCHAKE, JESS BULLER

Get your leadership team together with the cafeteria director and identify a day on the calendar when your team can take over. Make sure the menu is accommodating for you as well because YOU will be serving lunch that day. I like to shoot for chicken nuggets or corn dog day (let's be honest, you can't screw these up). Make a reservation at a local restaurant for your cafeteria staff and let them know the night before (or even surprise them). Then, send them out to lunch and assure them that your team has lunch under control. Your cafeteria staff will be very grateful and the students will love seeing you in a different role. Two things to remember here: 1) take plenty of pictures and share it on social media and; 2) make sure the restaurant knows you are picking up the tab so your staff isn't buying their own lunch!

SWAG (STUFF WE ALL GET)

In the perfect world I would give big pay raises and extended amounts of time off to every staffulty member each year. This, however, requires some elements of which I have no control. Add to it, most people in education are not simply motivated by money, not that money doesn't help. Looking for every opportunity to share some love doesn't require a lot of money, just a lot of creativity. SWAG is a great example. Swag can be shirts, stickers, pins, pencils. Come on, be real here — educators love stuff!

Every year I like to do a staffulty shirt or two and a few other fun things. I have done baseball jerseys where staffulty get to choose the number they want on the back. It is a great way to show unity and, depending on your district, a great excuse to wear jeans at work. Stickers with your school or district's catch phrase, hashtag, or logo are popular with those who like to decorate their laptops, water bottles, or car windows and bumpers.

TEACHER OF THE YEAR

An interesting twist leaders can do with naming a teacher of the year is to have staffulty and/or students provide the nominations. Another way to make this a special celebration of the staffulty is to announce all the nominees at a big public event. West Grand School District does an annual 'Celebration of Excellence'. At this spring event, students are showing off examples of their learning, projects, capstones, and their talents. This is a perfect time to shine the spotlight on all nominees and blow the roof off for the winner. Once your winner is announced, nominate them for the state teacher of the year. Take them to a conference, really honor them. Put a big plaque outside their classroom door, get their picture on social media and in the papers. You never know how far it will go. The first West Grand teacher of the year, Nellie Thomson, ended up being a finalist for the Colorado Teacher of the Year. The pride in our community was amazing.

LISTENING IS LOVING

Part of being the leader of your school is to be in classrooms. We've even created a new word for this practice. The walkthrough, right? Yeah, we walk through classrooms all the time, giving feedback and checking on the progress of whatever initiative we have launched that school year. This is a very good practice when done the right way. When they are done wrong or without a clear 'why' attached to them, they can be a disaster.

As important as being in the classroom when students are present might be, consider being in the classroom when the kids aren't there. This can happen in many different ways. There are definitely times when meeting with a teacher in the leader's office is more appropriate. But that should be the only time the leader's office is the chosen destination for meetings. When possible, leaders should go to the staffulty member's location rather than their own office. By simple appearance, summoning someone to your office implies your time to be more valuable than is theirs. Leaders have more flexibility in their schedules than teachers do. If a meeting is needed, schedule it for the teacher's prep time and go to their space. It will create a lot less angst and increases the time you are out and visible to others.

I'm an open book to my staffulty, they probably all have my cell phone number and know they can text or call me any time. I occasionally get a text or an email asking to meet with me. I will always ask when and tell them I will come to them for our meeting. Unless they have something very private, they are excited to have me come to their room. I once got an email from an elementary teacher asking to meet with me. I followed the usual protocol and set up time to go see her during the following week. I had been told by her principal she wanted to take an extra day off after a holiday. In my district, like many others, only the superintendent can approve this time off. I could have emailed then and said, no problem, time off granted. But instead, I kept the meeting. She shared her request, which I approved happily. It was the next thing that was impactful and left a lasting impression on me. I asked her, knowing she was having a tough year with some high behavioral and social-emotionally challenged students, a very basic question, *"How are you doing?"*

Her response began with biting her lip and tears welling in her eyes. The content of our conversation will remain between the two of us but it's important to never forget that sometimes people just want to have someone listen to them and demonstrate how much they care. My wife and daughter would confirm this, I'm an easy cry. Soon, both the teacher and I were in tears. We weren't looking for solutions, we were just sharing struggles and successes with our most at-risk students. At the end of the conversation I asked her what I could do to help. Her answer was "This. Just come listen to me."

"99% of the people we might label as resistant, struggling, or not on board just simply want to be heard."

• Laurie Kagan •

LEADING FROM A PLACE OF LOVE

Loving your staffulty is more than trinkets and notes. Being human and being vulnerable with them, treating them the way you'd want to be treated is not a magic formula. Rather it is simple common decency. If you want to motivate people, to lead people then begin from a place of love and they will follow you anywhere.

CHAPTER
SIX

CRANK UP THE RADIO WITH STUDENT VOICE AND ACTION

Leadership is not about top down decisions, but it's about caring for people and their dreams.

UNKNOWN

My first year as the building principal happened to coincide with one of 2011's most powerful and unstoppable forces, Tebowmania! Earlier that season the Broncos were struggling with a new head coach and a rather lacklustre roster. Fans wanted to see Tim Tebow, their prized 1st round pick from the previous year. With each Kyle Orton incompletion and subsequent loss, the pressure grew on head coach John Fox. Eventually, Fox gave the fans, including me, what they wanted - Tebow as the starting quarterback.

If you watched the NFL at that time, you know Tebow was, at best, average. In most of his starts he completed very few passes and often missed wide open receivers by a mile. Yet somehow, week after week, the Broncos would get a break here and there late in the game. Tebow-mania was alive and the Broncos were the most entertaining team in America. (as a fan I can tell you they were awful, but rather entertaining to watch) After each amazing play, and often on the sidelines, Tebow (a devout Christian) would take a knee, place his forehead on his fist, in an iconic pose dubbed 'the Tebow'.

The 'Tebow' began sweeping the nation and filled social media with photos and videos of adults and kids alike striking the pose. In many schools administrators began banning the move, calling it a disruption. Not this guy! I was frequently doing the Tebow in the front hallway with my kids. We even had the entire student body, and me, doing the Tebow late in a basketball game when we needed a free throw to win.

Often administrators won't have this type of interaction with their students. Some might delegate this to assistants or deans, maybe teachers. My question is always why? Why would you not want to be with your kids and have some fun, letting them see you as a human being and not some stuffy guy in a suit? I am guilty of taking myself too seriously at times during my principalship. I wore a suit nearly every day. But I never stopped making time to be with my kids, to listen to my kids, and to be there for them. The idea of this chapter is just that, being there for kids and activating them as the leaders they are...now!

YOU NEVER KNOW

I have a few catch phrases I use frequently without even noticing I do so. Odds are you do as well. It's important that we think about what we say and are intentional with our words. You never know who's listening and when something we say might make a difference.

Recently I was at a regional function for our area school districts. One of my colleagues pulled me aside to introduce me to someone who had taught with him in a different district. The teacher, Mikala, had been a student of mine for just one year, her freshman year, but remembered me for a specific event during that time. After connecting and her jogging my memory she told me the story of a low point for her and the role I had played. A story I didn't recall at the time but will now remember forever.

Due to some family issues, Mikala had a very tough time her freshman year and was angry at the world. The tipping point was one morning in the hallway when the words of another student sent her over the edge. She jumped in and started a fight with the other student, resulting in myself and one of my APs needing to separate the two. I rarely handled any discipline as the principal but this particular day only two administrators were in the school. My AP took the older student, I took Mikala. Fights in the hallway were rare by this point but our consequences were clear, 5 days out of school and the police would be issuing a citation. The process could be handled quickly and if the guy I told you about early in the book, myself as the AP, would have handled this he would have yelled at Mikala and kicked her out the door. Instead, I calmed her down and made sure she wasn't injured. But it was what I said, according to Mikala, that made the difference. As I left the room I told her something I have said to kids for quite some time. In fact, I say it frequently enough now I don't notice it.

Make good choices.

Hearing Mikala tell this story brought tears to my eyes and a big hug for Mikala. She went on to tell me that not only is she a teacher but painted on the wall in her classroom are quotes about making good choices. Again, you never know who's listening or when you'll say something that will impact another life. I'm proud of Mikala and who she's become. I know she's making good choices with her life.

TRUE STUDENT LEADERSHIP

As a junior high school student, I served as the campaign manager for a friend running for student class president. Ok, it seemed a lot cooler at the time and really felt important. The future of our 7th grade class hung in the balance after all. Well, I must not have been any good at my job because my guy didn't win and, somehow our class survived under the very capable leadership of someone else. Reflecting on it now, I have no clue what it would have meant for him to be class president, nor do I think most of my classmates did.

Truth be told, the role of student councils are important in schools and I don't mean to downplay the typical student council group. Yet, often we don't leverage the actual leadership skills these students have nor do we task our non-student council kids with leadership roles. Our students are capable and ready to be much more than figurehead leaders. They are ready to impact our communities and our schools now and we must allow them the opportunity to do so.

In my first year as a principal I had a student come and visit me in the summer asking to bring a speaker she'd heard at a leadership conference to our school. I am never opposed to letting our students hear from others and was curious. I'd never heard of Rachel's Challenge, a program developed by the parents of Rachel Scott, a victim of the Columbine school shooting. It would have been easy to simply say, 'yes let's do this' but instead I asked the student to begin putting in the work to bring the program to our school. It took some time and organization, but we were able to have a speaker from Rachel's Challenge at our school for all students and staffulty to experience. What a powerful time for our kids and adults, but more importantly for that student, a moment when she knew she was heard and given the opportunity to lead in our school and community.

Students bring ideas to us as leaders quite frequently. If this isn't happening we should be asking ourselves why. Is it possible we shot down a few too many ideas and word has spread? Do we have a culture in place that allows for student voice and opportunity to make an impact? Sometimes these might be smaller ideas, sometimes big ideas that have lasting impact. The key is not to say no to student concepts but rather to turn them into teachable moments.

TEACHABLE MOMENTS

This example comes from two middle school students at the West Grand K8 school. They approached their assistant principal and mentioned how they wished they had access to water bottles more frequently, especially after volleyball practice. The AP asked for a little more information and quickly saw they were asking for a vending machine for their school. This was not something that had been in place so he wasn't sure what to do. Rather than solve the problem for the students, or simply dismiss them as 7th grade kids, he asked them to put together a proposal for what they were thinking. The students did just that. They performed a simple survey of their student body and pitched their idea to me and members of the leadership cabinet. This was an awesome teachable moment for those two students, as they found the need to dive into USDA regulations, district policy, fire codes, and the like. While this took them several presentations, they ultimately were able to secure the vendor, appropriate beverages, and have the machine in place. It is still there today and students are grateful to be able to purchase water and a few other drinks during their day. While this might seem like just a vending machine, the powerful element behind it is students knowing they can bring ideas forward and make a difference in their school because adults are listening to them.

The second example came from a high school student while I was still at Rock Springs High. During a summer conference for the student council, she'd heard about another school providing food for disadvantaged students over the weekend. Knowing the challenges our community faced with families in poverty she saw an opportunity to make an impact. I encouraged her to run with the idea and, along with her career academy director's support, it became her senior capstone project. During a tour of our school with some community leaders, we stopped in the class as she was presenting her project. Before we left the room, she had commitments of money, in-kind donations, and pledges of support from the community leaders. The project began by supporting one of the elementary schools with backpacks loaded with meals for the weekend to send home with students. Even after her graduation, the project became one handed down year after year, and it now supports every elementary school in the community. Talk about impact from a high school student! When we encourage our kids instead of dismissing their ideas they can, and will, have tremendous impact.

This final example should say to us all (in flashing neon lights) PAY ATTENTION TO YOUR KIDS. Pay attention to what they say and what they do. Building relationships with your students will help them learn more about what you care about while at the same time unveiling equally, if not more, about them as human beings. I met Angel when he was a sophomore at West Grand High. Angel was a super involved student. He was on the cheer/pom squad, basketball team, ran track, was in student council, Renaissance leadership, art club, science fair, and more. During his time in high school, Angel and I had many conversations and I knew quite a lot about him. The thing I knew most about Angel was that he was one of the most talented artists I'd ever met. He was awarded multiple times by the Colorado State Science Fair the honor of designing their event program cover.

When you write a book, you reach a stage where you think, "Huh, I just might finish this thing!" It was around that time I began thinking about cover designs for my book. I am not, repeat NOT, an artist. I am the guy who cannot draw a straight line with a ruler. When the time came to move forward with cover design, I reached out to Angel and asked if he'd consider being my cover concept artist. If you read the copyright page, you'll know how that story ends.

STUDENT VOICE IN DECISION MAKING

When the team began to form at RSHS to address our school culture, we chose to focus on just a few things to fix. We knew many areas could be addressed. We chose to target attendance first. Our data showed one of the worst attended class periods was third. As adults, we were perplexed but began throwing out ideas about why this might be the case. We had a rather comprehensive list but decided we should talk with students and get their input. We put a team of kids together, by recommendation of their teachers, and asked for their thoughts. We learned a lot from this exercise, including, Adults don't have a clue what kids are thinking!

At least that's what we felt like. Even with all the items on our list behind poor third period attendance we had completely missed the mark. I honestly can't recall what was on our list, but what wasn't on the list was the top reason for students. They were hungry!

Sure, we saw them coming in with their coffee cups but didn't make the connection. So, why not look to provide snacks for our kids in the middle of the morning. It made a big difference in our attendance. It didn't solve the problem but it was a big step forward for us.

We leveraged the ideas of our students even more when we began having academic pep rallies. Ideas we had for themes were quickly dismissed by our kids because, well, adults just aren't cool. The kids really saved us and our efforts to improve the culture of the school. Imagine what would have happened had we not listened to our students and given them a voice to make a difference. The effort would have failed, miserably.

Having a student voice in decision making is essential and can be done in so many varied ways. As a principal, I had one student on the community Chamber of Commerce Board of Directors. The student was a voting member, not figuratively on the board. Working with the chamber director, we would select a student who could serve for a two-year term. As a superintendent, I have two students sitting on the District Accountability Committee, a committee required by state law. In this case, a middle school student and a high school student serve in a leadership role and carry the same weight as any parent, administrator, or teacher in the group.

As a district, we recently went through the process of developing our learner profile. We collected so much data through a variety of activities but none more important than those done with our students. Once the information was compiled, a

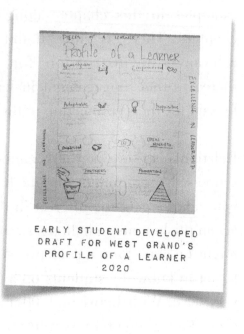

EARLY STUDENT DEVELOPED DRAFT FOR WEST GRAND'S PROFILE OF A LEARNER 2020

group of high school students were tasked with creating prototypes for the profile. They created four very unique concepts which were shared with our staffulty, the accountability committee, the board of education, and the leadership team. A smaller group of students then worked through all the feedback and developed the final draft of our learner profile. The buy-in from the entire community on this document comes simply from the student-driven nature of the project.

STUDENT OWNERSHIP PAYOFF

If the goal of education is really about student learning, it is imperative that leaders do everything possible to connect students to their schools. I've shared many examples in this chapter along with others in prior chapters. There is little doubt that increasing the relevance of instruction for students drastically increases their engagement in learning. The same can be said for their connection to their schools.

Relationships are key to connecting kids to their schools. Every student should have at least one adult who takes a genuine interest in them and notices their accomplishments, challenges, and even when they might be gone for a day or two. As the principal, I tried to get to know my students on a first name basis at the very least. With between 1200 and 1400 students each year during my tenure, plus a fairly high transient population, this wasn't always possible. I would try to have at least 75% of their names down by the end of the year. Freshman were the most difficult to learn due to not having any disciplinary responsibilities. I mostly learned their names by being in classrooms and at events.

Jeremy was the exception when it came to freshman. He was a tough kid, a kid like so many of us have met. Jeremy was foul mouthed, disobedient, and had little to no interest in school. He was hard to be around, had very poor hygiene, and yet somehow I knew who he was early in the year. That might be from the time he spent in my APs office, which was quite a bit of time. Every kid needs love at school, some need it more than others. Jeremy desperately needed our love!

I made an intentional effort to build a relationship with Jeremy, starting with simply calling him by his name in the hallway. Just saying hi to him every day was important to me. I had high hopes for Jeremy but was realistic knowing he had a challenging home life. As the year went by, Jeremy progressed from a head nod in the halls to stopping and saying hi. I can't say he made any headway in the classroom but, you know, baby steps. I sat in my office (the front hall) with Jeremy towards the end of his freshman year and asked, 'Hey what's the plan? Do you see yourself graduating from high school?' Jeremy told me he didn't have any use for school and once he turned 16 he was out the door. This was hard to hear — clearly just saying hi wasn't going to be enough to move the needle with him.

As we entered his sophomore year, Jeremy was much more open with me (we even had our own handshake) but made still no attempt to pass classes. He had started the year with maybe 1 credit, not sure how he'd passed a class but still he had 1. Only 23 to go. I knew Jeremy would turn 16 later in the year and was hoping to turn him around. A few weeks into the year I was looking into student grades and reviewing the 'F' list. I noticed a name missing from the list, Jeremy's name. I quickly looked to see if I had missed something, maybe he had transferred out or switched to the alternative school. Nope, there he was on my screen - and he was passing EVERYTHING!

I had made a difference right? Not really. Turns out Jeremy decided he needed to turn things around after he landed himself on probation. If he were to avoid being sent to the boy's school, he had to pass his classes. And he was — and he saw success he didn't know he could have at school. I praised him, was extra enthusiastic with the handshake, but Jeremy still intended to drop out. He just had to make it through probation. But for that year, Jeremy would be a better student, or good enough to stay under the judge's radar. Jeremy even went to summer school and recovered a credit he'd lost as a freshman.

Junior year came and Jeremy was still getting by, but just barely. He was tired all the time and missed a few days here and there. Early in second semester I was manning my usual spot in the front hall and realized I hadn't seen Jeremy in quite a few days. I asked my APs if they'd seen him but they hadn't. The probation agent happened to be in the hall and pulled me aside. Jeremy, she told me, was in jail. It turned out a few family members had been using Jeremy as their drug mule, having him drive the 2 plus hours to Salt Lake City a few times per week in the evening. It started to make sense. But this time, it wasn't just Jeremy. Those family members were also in jail with him.

I love you and I believe in you - you're going to be ok.

The next day, I saw Jeremy in the front hall and, as the bell rang, he came straight toward me rather than turning right, heading to his Science class. "Pep, we need to talk...NOW," Jeremy said. We sat in the front hall where, through his tears, he told me the whole story. He was being asked, as the only juvenile in his case, to testify against his family. He also had to graduate, on time, in order to avoid jail time himself. He looked at me desperate for advice. I had none to give. Instead, I said the only thing I knew to say. "Jeremy, I love you and I believe in you — you're going to be ok."

Jeremy had the hard decision to make. Mine was only to try and build a plan, along with his counselor, to help him graduate. He needed a small miracle but we are educators! Miracles are our specialty, right!?

The beginning of Jeremy's senior year brought a different kid to our school. He was bright-eyed, wore clean clothes, had showered, even his hair was combed. Jeremy was fired up to take on the challenge. He had aced summer school and with a lot of other online courses, credit recovery classes, and a full load he was on track to make it to graduation. I was proud of Jeremy and I let him know every chance I could. Our handshake had been replaced with a hug. He was even recognized in our academic pep rally! The looks on his friends' faces were priceless. He beamed with pride. I teared up as did many others. Two days to go, Jeremy was on track and had only one big assignment left. This last hurdle was a term paper in his English class but Jeremy assured me as he left school the night it was due that he had it in the bag. "Heck Pep, it's almost done and it will be in before midnight".

I was in the hallway the next morning just a few minutes into the day when Jeremy came up the stairs. Freshman Jeremy was back — cussing, angry, ready to storm out the door one final time. He calmed down enough to share with me how his paper was not in by midnight and his teacher had said, "Too bad, see you in summer school." Jeremy was destroyed, I was flabbergasted. How could this be? He had the thing basically done. Even a mostly completed paper should have been enough to get him across the line. I went and visited with his teacher and asked for her side of the story. Jeremy hadn't turned in the paper until after 4am and her deadline was midnight. All or nothing. I proceeded to ask the teacher what she knew about Jeremy. She told me he was a troublemaker and had done nothing for her as a freshman or a sophomore so she wasn't surprised by this lack of meeting a deadline.

There are times, as a leader, when we have to balance personalities, right and wrong, adult and student dynamics. I support my teachers. Sometimes, though, we are just plain wrong. We all make mistakes and, in this case, the mistake was not even knowing Jeremy's story. I shared his story, all of it. Including the call I had gotten that morning from his probation officer telling me Jeremy's family had been released from jail the night before and had caused huge problems at Jeremy's foster home. I understood why he might have been a little late with the paper and now, through her tears, she did as well. Jeremy got an A on that paper and made it to graduation.

We started a tradition a few years before this time in which all seniors wore a white stole around their neck at graduation. Written on the inside of the stole was a message of gratitude from the senior to the person who made a difference in their journey to graduation. Occasionally, a student would ask for two, wanting to give one to mom and one to dad who had divorced prior to graduation. I had parents, grandparents, and others who would tell me stories in public about receiving the stole and how much it meant to them.

Every stole has an amazing story...and I have Jeremy's stole.

SEVEN

FULL SPEED AHEAD: BEING THE AUTHOR OF THE STORY

If you don't tell your story someone else will, and you probably won't like their version of the story.

UNKNOWN

When the phone rang, I was fairly certain I knew why. Our girls basketball team had just lost their first round game at the state tournament. It had been one of those games; the girls didn't play well, they struggled to hit shots, and officiating was questionable, or at least our fans thought so. I was at the game, as I always was for the tournament. The coach was under some fire and had several unhappy parents. You get the picture.

Answering the phone, I heard the voice of one of my staff members who had listened to the game over the radio back at home. It was really awesome that our local radio station had a person who broadcast all our home and away games over the airwaves, further showing the passion that town has for its school and its sports. The announcer, we will call him John, exemplified those characteristics but played jump rope with the line between passion and inappropriateness for an announcer. During our girl's loss he had gone well over the line and I was being asked to do something about it.

Earlier in the season, John had invited me to join him for the halftime show on a Friday night. We had a great conversation about some of the great things happening at our school (yes, here is another awesome way to tell your school's story) and about how the season was progressing. John concluded our interview by offering an open invitation to do color commentary any time I wanted. As I saw John leaving the arena after our first round loss, I casually said, "Hey John, put those headphones out for me tomorrow, I'd love to join you."

For the duration of the tournament, maybe four games combined for girls and boys, I did color commentary on the radio. I found John a very different announcer when I was at the table with him. His complaining about officiating, coaching decisions, and disgust when players made mistakes seemed to dissipate. When the tournament ended, several staff and community members texted or called thanking me for being on the radio. I knew it wasn't my riveting basketball insight they appreciated. Sometimes, a leader needs to step up and control the message.

BUYING THE RHETORIC

When asked, an alarmingly high percentage of people will say schools in America are not getting the job done. Yet, when asked about their own local schools, the level of confidence is higher. Why might this be? The average person will report higher quality at their local school compared to schools nationally. Two reasons honestly prevail. First, it is quite possible the person responding has at least one child in the local school system and has had a favorable experience. Second, national news stories about schools are rarely positive and often focus on cutting programs like the arts and physical education. Local news may tell a more positive story about the schools, but we aren't usually that newsworthy. Unless we choose to make ourselves newsworthy.

Most communities rally behind their schools and in many cases are still filled with people who either attended the schools themselves or had/have children in the school district. What about the people in the community who don't have kids coming into the buildings each day, are you doing anything to include them in your work? Think about a small business in your community, any small business. Got one in mind? Good!

Now think about the owner of that business. They don't have kids in the school district. So where do they get information about your schools? Might they be basing their perception on how kids behave in their establishment? In reality, people carry many perceptions and beliefs about the schools in their towns and neighborhoods based on rumor, second hand stories, and what they read online.

SHARE YOUR STORY

I recently spent a day with a principal friend at his local high school. He was having a difficult time with the perceptions people have of his school. They are wildly successful in athletics! They are in the running for, or winning, the state title in every sport. It is super impressive.

As we walked around on the tour, I was introduced to many teachers, students, and other staffulty. The principal had told me he needed help moving some of his staff forward and was facing a lot of resistance. I heard some of that but also witnessed some moments of greatness. I was struck with how amazing their

Junior Reserve Officer Training Program (JrROTC) is both from an enrolment perspective and by the pride the students have in the program. A quick stop in the health occupations classroom uncovered another gem, with students working on phlebotomy certifications and actually 'sticking' needles in visitors and their peers. Other cool things included a student creating a case for their phone with the 3D printer, another creating artwork in the welding shop, and one of the best math bingo games I've ever seen. Yet, when we got back to his office the principal was completely focused on the negativity he was faced with as his big obstacle.

Much like my life before the two questions, he was so focused on what his staff was doing wrong that he could not see all the things they were getting right. And their stories needed to be told. The challenge he was faced is familiar to most leaders. We allow ourselves to get caught up on negative voices instead of focusing on those powerful stories. Leaders, we can't let others form opinions without all the facts. Instead, let's broadcast and celebrate the incredible stories happening daily in our schools.

MAKING POSITIVE CONNECTIONS

I used to be the teacher who used red ink. I marked up papers with the best of them, including the big -24, -11, or whatever number of incorrect answers were on the paper. A simple flip to writing +36, + 29, or the number they got right was a huge change for me and my students. As Rita Pierson once said, "-18 sucks all the life out of you. +2 says I ain't all bad."

It isn't the easiest thing to do, shifting your mind from looking for things that are wrong to seeking out the positives. But it's worth it. It becomes a habit the more you do it too. Try this when walking in the halls of your schools. Never let a student or an adult pass your face without saying hi or paying them a compliment. If a student has a concert t-shirt on, mention the band. If you don't know the band, ask about it. Say something about their shoes, backpack, something. Can't find something then just say hi, good morning, how are you, or it's good to see you today. I never let someone cross my face without acknowledging them. It keeps the human connection in place and lets them know I see them and I value them as people.

TELLING THE STORY

This next section is designed to be quick-hitting with ideas of how you might tell your school or district's story. Included in this chapter are ways to leverage social media and to get kids involved in the storytelling process. But first, let's talk about marketing and branding.

If you'd have told me back in 1995 when I first started in education that I'd need to market and brand my school, classroom, or team, I would have laughed. Let's be honest, unless you actually studied business in college this is probably an area in which you haven't the first clue where to begin. I know I certainly never got any training in my masters or doctoral programs that would have been of benefit.

COMMANDING SOCIAL MEDIA

Among the easiest methods to tell your story is through social media. Nearly everyone has a device in their hand and are never far away from the screen. So take advantage of that and push the message you want being repeated. The key to social media is identifying who your target audience is and where they hangout.

If parents are your focus, hit them on Facebook. I began my Facebook journey, as it pertains to schools, when I was the building principal. I opened a Facebook page and branded it a certain way. The title of the page was Rock Springs High School (Authentic). I was asked often what the 'authentic' meant. At that time, 2011, not every school had their own page and often people had created fake pages. My school was no different and I wanted people to know that we were the AUTHENTIC page for Rock Springs High. I started with a couple of picture posts, our student/leaders of the week, and began to get a decent following. But then, I hit the motherload of Facebook posts and the number of followers skyrocketed.

Wyoming holds their state spirit competition the day before and in the same location as the 3A and 4A basketball tournaments. Being the dance dad I am, I chose to be the administrator to attend state spirit. Armed with my new Facebook page, I videoed the performances of both the cheer squad and the Tiger Rhythm Dance Team (TRDT) and posted them to the page. Within an hour those posts had more than 10x the number of views as we had people following the page (at the time we maybe had 800 followers). By the time the evening ended, over 11,000 views for each of TRDT's performances, and nearly that many for cheer. At that point, any and everything that could be done via video went to the page in that fashion. If I saw something cool in a classroom, I recorded it and on the page it went. Facebook Live has brought this into another realm. Protip: I share everything we post on our district Facebook page, HS page, and K8 page on my personal Facebook timeline. It's an easy way to amplify the message and to grow your followers on the school/district page.

If your target audience is your kids, Facebook won't cut it. Our kids are on Instagram, SnapChat, and Tik Tok. A big key is how you are telling the story to kids compared to parents. The things they have in common (seeing themselves/their kids, ease of access, sharing themselves/their kids with their followers) are trumped by where they actually spend their time.

If the goal is to make it a promotion for your school or district, or to use your message as a recruitment tool, LinkedIn is probably the medium you're looking for. I rarely use LinkedIn for telling our school's story. It is great for personal business (#PepTalks, Road To Awesome work) but it seems to fall short as it relates to schools.

Twitter (my favorite platform) is also one we don't find many parents or kids using and, thus, I don't tell much of the school story here. Twitter, however, is the best place for professional growth and networking, as you'll see coming up in Chapter 8.

THE ART OF THE HASHTAG

When you search the history of the hashtag you'll find the name Chris Messina attached and credited with its evolution. Chris felt the internet, and specifically Twitter, needed a method for organizing information and categorizing tweets. The use and importance of hashtags has grown tremendously since that August day in 2007 when Messina first tweeted the suggestion that ended the pound sign and converted it to a hashtag.

Today, it is difficult to find posts on Twitter that do not have a hashtag attached. Hashtags are more than just placeholders, they are almost a fashion statement. They are a way of adding flair, of putting a stamp on your social media post. So, what about your hashtag? How can you find that perfect fit for your personal story or your school? I may sound a bit repetitive, but hit your core values. What describes your personal story best? The #RoadToAwesome is all about my journey. It began with a guy wandering around clueless about his future and has evolved into someone passionate about growing leaders and following the positive path. Some of my favorite personal ones connect to who the person is just as much to what they do for a living. Take Bethany Hill, an elementary administrator in Arkansas. She started the #JoyfulLeaders movement several years ago and that connects to exactly who she is as a leader and as a person. Jonathan Alsheimer is a rockstar teacher in Virginia and wrote the book Next Level Teaching. He truly does everything at the 'next level' and his hashtag #NextLevelTeaching describes him, his book, and how he leads and loves in and out of the classroom perfectly. Dwight Carter, a school administrator in Ohio uses #BeGreat. If you know Dwight or have heard him speak, his message and his persona are about our own greatness and making the choice to #BeGreat.

When I was the principal in Rock Springs, our school used the hashtag #ProudToBeATiger. So many in the community had attended and graduated from that high school that it was truly a pride point. Many schools have their spirit days or wear their school colors on Fridays. In Rock Springs, the entire community wears

#PROUDTOBEATIGER BY
ERIKKA SOTO
ROCK SPRINGS HIGH
2015

black and orange on Fridays. When I came to West Grand the brand had already begun with #WeAreWestGrand. Again, a community very proud of their heritage and their schools. We've taken the hashtag here and developed fully into our brand.

We worked hard to brand our school. The mascot is the tiger and one of our students began using a hashtag on social media. I asked her to paint it in our hallway. That had become a huge part of who we were.

Hashtags are easy to create and can be quite catchy. If you want one that is going to align with your brand and stick, keep three things in mind. First, make sure the hashtag describes yours or your school's values in some fashion. Second, it should represent what riding for your brand means. Finally, it should be unique and identifiable to you. My alma mater, University of Wyoming, is a perfect example for how you build a hashtag to fit who you are and what you represent. The state of Wyoming is very proud and, with only one 4 year university, everyone identifies with the brown and gold, the bucking horse and rider, and the Cowboy lifestyle. The hashtag for not only UW but for the state is simple and beautiful. #GoWyo That's how it's done.

What hashtag fits and distinguishes you and your school?

NARRATING THE STORY

My daughter's best friend in high school has a little brother named Tyson. He is one of the most entertaining people you'll ever meet and he's a YouTube star. Even though he is just a grade school kid, he has well over 300 subscribers to his channel. He makes silly videos and uploads them to his YouTube page. Yes, having a YouTube show is in fact that easy! I took Tyson's idea and ran with it. No, I don't make silly videos but instead I use the platform to tell my school district's stories. I host a show I call the #WeAreWestGrand Talk Show. (see what I did there with the hashtag??) I schedule a teacher, student, administrator or whomever about once a month and we sit and talk for about 15 minutes. A little bit of quick editing and I have a show. This gets pushed out to the YouTube channel, our Facebook page, and through our parent/student portal. On the show, I've hosted the entire wrestling team (pee wee through high school); a middle school girl who started a donation charity called 'The Closet', where students can donate or receive clothing, toys, shoes, and other items; the cast and directors of the high school play; the robotics team, and even those two students who were responsible for our first vending machine!

MY 2ND GRADE MOVE

When I was in the 2nd grade my parents decided it was time to upgrade from the old trailer park and our family double-wide. Mom and dad looked at many different houses and neighborhoods in my hometown of Casper before deciding on the house that became my childhood home. There were certain requirements mom had for choosing our family home, including the elementary and junior high schools her three kids would attend. Our new neighborhood put us in the same elementary school and junior high area as that which our mom had attended.

It is not uncommon for people to choose where they buy their homes based on the schools in the area. Much of what people know about our schools comes from web searches and from conversations with their realtor. If you want them to know the whole story, don't rely on some website that rates schools based on surveys taken by angry folks or based solely on test scores. Instead, do this: invite your area realtors to a meeting with you and a few of your leadership team. Cater lunch in (use your culinary program if you have one) and just talk with them. Listen to their ideas and answer questions they might have about your school or district. Realtors are very smart, very well connected folks — they can help you tell your school's story. Give them the chance, partner up with them. They can also help you when you might need housing for a new hire.

LETTING YOUR CULTURE TELL THE STORY TO FUTURE STAFFULTY

I attend a lot of job fairs all around the country. From my perspective not many people are Googling my town and seeking to move to our little slice of heaven. That certainly has nothing to do with how desirable the location is, quite the contrary. Many people want to move to and live in the mountain west, they just don't know about us. My job is to sell them on either starting or continuing their careers with us in Grand County.

But everyone else in the room has the same charge. We are there to recruit and it is competitive.

While attending a job fair recently, I noticed a trend and decided it was time to buck against it. As I looked around the ballroom playing host to this particular event, suits were everywhere. Some very expensive, some not so much. Everyone dressed to the hilt, including the candidates. I appreciate the candidates bringing their A game, but there is a near zero percent chance they dress this way once they hit the trenches of the teaching world. I cannot say I wasn't one of them also suited up, I was for sure. But it was time for a change.

Recruiting is about telling your school or district's story. It is an art, selling someone on spending a part of their life in your community. Yet, today's generation of new teachers aren't looking for the guy in the suit. They aren't concerned about the retirement package or any other traditional benefits. I can offer them a four day work week, free skiing on Fridays, and a small town, small district atmosphere. But what they really want is to know if they have advancement opportunities. Will they be able to continue their own education? What type of supports will be available for their professional growth? Most importantly, today's new teacher wants to know about the culture of your district and school.

Who better to tell them than your most important stakeholders, your staffulty and your students? Our employment website, designed by someone in the same generation, is composed of pictures of our staffulty and students doing the things they love most in our community and county. Each picture is hyperlinked to a site that tells you more about that activity. Prospective new hires get to see the people they will teach next door to and with whom they will build relationships. They see kids they will have in their classrooms. The best part, the video in the center of the page, developed and created by our students, giving a tour of the district and community and interviewing kids and staffulty. The intentional message is that even though we are small, we are excellent. The underlying message that hits the culture of our district is one that honors everyone, includes everyone, and is something very special. After all, #WeAreWestGrand!

COMMUNICATING IN CRISIS

Some leaders may disagree with my points about telling the story of our schools. However, in times of crisis there can be no question about the importance of communication. These might be small events, like a medical emergency in the hallway, or a big event that might force a lockdown, shelter in place, or evacuation. Rarely will leaders receive criticism for not sharing something they saw in a classroom. But, leave a gap in communication or lack timeliness around a crisis and there is blood in the water.

Lunch was less than fifteen minutes away when the counselor knocked on Scott's door. I had been working with Scott in a consulting capacity for a few months and was on his campus that day for some next steps. The counselor informed him there had been an accident in the back parking lot and EMS was on the scene. Grabbing the radio, out the door Scott and I went, ready for action.

This particular high school campus is unique in that it has a fairly substantial population but only one exit from the student parking lot. That exit is where the accident had taken place. The victim was a parent of one of the schools' students and, while not seriously injured, would have to be transported by EMS. The lunch bell was now less than ten minutes away. Checking with law enforcement it was clear to Scott his entry/exit wouldn't be cleared in time for lunch, but he was able to negotiate one-way exiting traffic. Scott assigned his counselor and campus security for traffic control and turned back to me to fill me in. What might be the next steps he should be taking before the bell rings?

My suggestions to Scott were these:

- Have your other counselor get the student of the parent in the accident, ASAP, so they can be notified and not hear second hand.
- Have your front desk make an all-call and let students know what is happening so they are patient in the lot
- Push a message out so all parents/kids are aware and you can control the message.
- Call your superintendent — they need to be aware (Scott ran out so fast he forgot his phone) — have your AP call the superintendent.
- Walk casually from car to car as kids are driving out, let them know about the delay, and just visit — check seatbelts, be a dad (actually Scott's daughter is a student there and we saw her driving out too).

Scott absolutely CRUSHED this communication!! Later, when meeting with his superintendent, who complimented him and said it was the single-best communication they'd experienced as a superintendent or as a parent (the superintendent also has a daughter at the school).

As I write this book, we are living through the novel Coronavirus pandemic of 2020. Responding to communication needs during this time has been one of the most unique times I have ever experienced. The initial communications about closing our school doors and transitioning to online learning models were fairly routine and mundane. As time went on, it was important to shift what that communication looked like and its focus. As a leadership team, our focus was to support parents and students more than it was to inform them or tell our school's story. We shifted to telling more of our own stories, inviting people virtually into our homes. A daily video from a member of the leadership team was pushed out to parents and students. Topics varied from struggles we had with educating our children from home to simply giving yourself grace and finding joy. One leader did an entire series on learning something new, for him it was baking. These efforts have brought our community closer with our leaders and allowed us to further show the human beings we are outside of our leadership lives.

TELL YOUR STORY, OR SOMEONE ELSE WILL

Leaders have so many different roles they play. The role of the school leader has changed dramatically over the past ten or fifteen years. Among the duties that have evolved most during that time is being the narrator of the story. It is no longer enough to manage people, budgets, and curriculum. School leaders must be the face of their organization and be quite adept in marketing and communicating the reality of their organizations. George Couros famously said, "We need to make the positives so loud that the negative becomes almost impossible to hear." Your presence, use of social media, communication, and focus on finding stories that need to be told will keep you in position to be the author of the story.

CHAPTER
EIGHT

KEEPING IT BETWEEN THE LINES: THE CASE FOR COACHING

A good coach always coaches to a leader's potential, not his current level of performance. A good leadership coach will see the potential in you and inspire you accordingly.

ANDY STANLEY

The game was tied, 53-53 with just 3 seconds remaining in overtime. As the ball was tipped out of bounds under our basket, I turned to my assistant coach, Danny, asking if I had a timeout. Calmly he said, "Just run your best inbounds play here." I looked to my point guard Tennil, and signalled the play. Rachel, who the play was designed for, glanced at me with a little smile. As the players began moving and Rachel came off her screen, Tennil hit her in the hands (up high), perfect for a catch and shoot play. As the ball left Rachel's hand my hands went into the air, celebrating the victory before the ball had even gone through the net. SWISH! At the horn, ballgame over! In that moment, Danny was the best coach I could have had — he kept me calm, gave me advice, and helped all of us be successful.

Being an assistant principal meant I was not able to continue coaching. So I transferred my love of basketball from coaching to being the game announcer. The view from the scorer's table is amazing. You are right on the mid-court stripe and in the middle of the action. What I found though, was that I couldn't see every bit of the game because I was stationary in my seat. As a coach I was able to move around a little bit so the view was better. Once I became the principal I gave up this role to be 'more available'. The gym at my high school has a floor level and a balcony level. Standing at floor level is a different view than that from the balcony. I kind of wished I could have coached from that level. It is amazing what you can see when you're on the balcony looking down on the action. I could read defenses so much quicker. I could identify patterns in offensive plays as well as small changes in how a player was shooting the ball or seeing the floor.

The same is true in leadership. As leaders we are do-ers. We want to be in the middle of the action and involved in the day to day work, and we should be, right? But there comes a point when as a leader you have to be able to see the big picture, 'the view from the balcony' so to speak. As a leader, spending time on the balcony is essential to long term success in the organization. Often we will have some form of strategic plan or goals for the course of a school year. This equates well to the game plan a coach puts in place for an upcoming game. When it comes time for the game, the coach trusts the players to execute the plan. The coach will make some adjustments from the sidelines working to reach the best outcome - a win.

After the game, I would pop in the game film and be able to see the game from the balcony where our camera was positioned. This wasn't just watching the game but rather it was focusing on certain aspects that went well or areas where we struggled. Being a school leader is very similar to being a sports coach. Yet, as leaders we often get so caught up in the work that we forget to stop and watch the game film.

BALCONY LEADERSHIP

As a principal, I found myself standing on the balcony of our main gym looking down at the floor. It wasn't during a game either. I'm talking about times when the gym was empty and I could be alone with my thoughts. After I started working with Tom and became clearer about what my work really was, I realized I had to set time aside and actually reflect on my progress. The analogy of the balcony was so strong for me that I could look down at the floor and see in my mind's eye those things I held most important in my role. These balcony sessions were essential for me to monitor that which I believed to be essential.

- RELATIONSHIPS AND INTERACTIONS: Was I making the connections I needed to make with my kids in the building? Had I missed out on opportunities to meet new students in my school or to thank someone for something they had done to really represent our brand well? Who was I missing when talking with staffulty on their prep time? What relationships do I need to repair? Which ones are going well? What about parents, community, my business partners? Who do I need to make sure I check in with soon?

- SYSTEMS AND THEIR CONNECTIONS: What was going well and what was a challenge on the operational side of the house? What successes are we having on the academic side? Are my systems working well together? What might need a tune-up?

- PRESSURES: What might be pushing on me from above? What pressure am I getting from below? How am I balancing my life and my job? How might I leverage pressure to impact one of the systems in a positive manner?

- CLIMATE AND CULTURE: What might I need to do to keep morale high or to give it a boost? How is everyone feeling and what am I seeing from them? Are there tough conversations that need to be had to keep the climate and culture where I want it to be?

- STORYTELLING: When did we last push positive information and stories about our school, our kids, our staffulty? Is there something happening in the community or within our walls I need to be ahead of or addressing to keep negative information from owning the space?

You can imagine my time on the balcony was never just a few minutes but rather a series of 30-60 minute reflections. Occasionally I would take my laptop with me so it looked like I was typing or catching up on email. You never need to justify spending quality time on reflection. A few times students even asked about it and I shared freely what I was thinking. A powerful bit of vulnerability with kids that goes a long way when they understand how introspective you are about your work and in turn, their success.

You might also note the work, the REAL work, was where I spent my intentional time on the balcony. Relationships (staffulty and students), Systems &

Connections (vision), Pressure (vision and culture/climate), Culture and Climate, and Storytelling. My keys, the keys, to game changing school leadership. Don't waste balcony time on things that aren't important — focus and reflect on your core values!

COACHING FOR GROWTH AND SUCCESS

As a leader, your job is to create an environment where growth and success are not just possible but rather inevitable. The work of a leader isn't just checking items off a to do list. Leaders need to inspire, instil passion, and build people. YES, build people. This cannot happen when every interaction is evaluative. For growth to happen, for success to happen, we must embrace the belief that all victories begin with a loss, a failed attempt, or a moment when we couldn't do it...yet.

Raise your hand if you've heard about the Power of Yet. Well, of course you have. After all, the concept of growth mindset is not new. Many schools around the country talk about instilling that growth mindset and building what Angela Duckworth calls 'grit'. But how do we grow this in adults and how can we best encourage adults to grow it in kids? I believe it comes first and foremost from modeling. This is where I will pound my fist on the table and argue with anyone that coaching is essential for leaders to grow and be their best.

WHY COACHING ISN'T EMBRACED

There is a rather interesting phenomenon that exists not only in education but across the spectrum related to leadership. Nearly all leaders have worked their way up through the ranks of various roles to become a principal, superintendent, or whatever the title. This is a result of hard work, continued education, and a lot of success along the way. Yes people rise into greater leadership positions as a result of their track record.

Success in one role, however, does not predict success in the next. The required knowledge may be there but the support and on-the-job training necessary for greatness doesn't exist. It is just assumed that because one was a great operator they will be a great foreman. Why would someone who was a super teacher not automatically be amazing as the principal? Well, simple. The jobs are different! When these supports are offered in the form of coaching or mentoring, they may be rejected for fear of appearing weak or unable to perform up to the expectations of others.

The beliefs many carry about coaching are varied and often seen as something unnecessary. Some will view coaching as 'just for people who are new' or for 'struggling team members'. It can sometimes be seen as the precursor to being fired, like some last-ditch effort to save a bad employee. As a leadership coach, I was once asked why I was being paid to 'teach the principal how to do his job'. This view of coaching is outdated and does not fit at all with a growth mindset.

Other reasons why coaching may be viewed as either unnecessary or a luxury connect to resources a school or district might have available. These may be time, money, or even the personnel to perform such coaching. Consulting coaches are typically not as expensive as some may believe and can alleviate the personnel and time factors. Outside coaches bring no preconceived notions, relationships, or agendas to their role. These independent coaches also have no evaluative role, leaving them open to asking questions and not telling principals what to do. A coach can provide genuine feedback and keep the focus on growth and success.

COACHING LEADERS FOR GROWTH AND SUCCESS

Much like an instructional coach would have a cycle for coaching teachers, a coaching cycle is appropriate for leaders as well. Many varied models exist for these coaching cycles and most of them are outstanding. The model and the turnaround for feedback looks a little different.

LEADERSHIP COACHING CYCLE

- STEP 1: Initial observation - this is typically best done in a full or half day of shadowing the leader. Asking a lot of questions will help develop clarity of priorities and values. While this is an initial step, it is not replicated in the cycle after the initial observation. Additionally, the coach will have many conversations with teachers, office staff, assistant principals, counselors, students, and others. It is important to establish trust and build a relationship.

- STEP 2: Defining and Working on 'the work' - the purpose of this step is to identify what the leader holds as core values, what they view as the important work, and to help frame what work really matters and is impactful. This is an important step and should be revisited annually

- STEP 3: Leader self-assessment and feedback - in this step, the leader identifies what they see as their strengths, where they need to grow, and what current successes and stressors exist. Combining feedback from the coach's discussions with staffulty and students with the leader's self-assessment further inform the leader and the coach.

- STEP 4: Goal Setting - based on the previous step, the leader should identify two or three goals to focus on for a short cycle (defined as 3-6 weeks).

- STEP 5: Regular Check-In - the coach and leader schedule a regular time for an hour to have either face to face or phone and video calls. This is a time for the leader to share progress toward goals and struggles/successes since the last visit. These are typically weekly or every other week.

- STEP 6: Observation Loop - during the cycle, an in-person observation from the coach, including discussions with staffulty and students, further informs on progress the leader is making toward their goals. This also provides opportunity for adjustment to goals.

- STEP 7: Self-assessment - in this step, the leader assesses themselves on their goals and on their strengths and growth areas, noting changes and improvements. This is a great step for celebrating!

- Looping for continuous growth - return to step 3

6 AREAS LEADERS BENEFIT FROM COACHING

When thinking about leadership coaching it is best to focus on broad categories rather than trying to hone in on every behavior a leader might exhibit on a daily basis. As an early career principal I had a few areas that were really big hurdles for me. Tom, my coach, identified very quickly how I was ineffective with my calendar, delegating and trusting others, and having very few systems in place that would have improved work. Each leader is unique in their needs and has different experiences and mentors under which they learned and experienced leadership. Working from a basis of research, both mine as well as the research of others, there are five areas in which all leaders can benefit from coaching.

1. TIME MANAGEMENT: Being the leader of an organization, regardless of size, will lead to heavy demands on your time. I was asked by an early career principal once how, as she put it, I "did it all". The answer was simple, I didn't do it all. But early in my career I felt the need to do it all and to be everything to everyone. The secret to time management is having clear priorities. Sure, other things such as the use of an electronic calendar, cell phone reminders, and the like are effective, but if you are not clear on what your priorities are it is difficult to know what to put on that calendar. Much like knowing your core values will drive the work on which you focus, having priorities in your day to day and through your year will help put the important things on the calendar and ensure they get accomplished.

2. OPERATIONAL MANAGEMENT: By no stretch of the imagination are the operational parts of being the leader exciting or going to lead to time in the spotlight. Yet, if leaders are not focused on operational work along with the instructional leadership elements they might be doomed to failure. To put a little more definition on operational management, consider the following:

- BUDGET & RESOURCE MANAGEMENT - Every school district will do this differently. Leaders may have varied levels of control on their budgetary dollars but being disconnected from where and how money is aligned with the priorities and values of the leader can lead to miscommunication and a lack of trust from staffulty. Spend the time needed to understand and build a budget that is meaningful and that others understand and can take ownership of. Rather than simply telling teachers they will get the same dollar amount each year, ask what they might need. Build a system by which budgetary dollars can be shared through the school to meet those needs from year to year. This increase in transparency and collaboration will lead to better communication and a feeling of being valued and heard.

- SCHEDULE - This might include the day to day schedule, master schedule, specials rotations, or even the duty schedule for everyone. If leaders make the assumption that everyone will be where they are expected to be at all times but haven't invested the time to gather understanding and support around the schedules, a disaster may be lurking around the next corner.

- TEAM COORDINATION - Every leader loves to go to meetings, right? No, of course not. These meetings however, are a part of the role that is often overlooked. I have worked with many leaders who say things like, "I don't have regular meetings because I really respect my team's time." Truth, I have been one of those people. While I don't encourage any leader to hold meetings for the sake of holding meetings, when a lack of information is present a vacuum is created. That vacuum is almost exclusively filled with misinformation requiring an excessive amount of time to correct. I agree that if the information can come in an email, then send it in an email. Regular meetings in smaller groups, maybe by department, custodial staff, lead teachers, or with the office staff give the face to face time needed to clarify and keep everyone focused on the goals and mission at hand. Every leader needs to experiment with the frequency and structure of these meetings, however, the importance of being available to answer questions and listen to your staff cannot be overlooked.

- HUMAN RESOURCES - Hiring and onboarding new staffulty is a small part of what school leaders do but when done well it will have a strong impact on the school. Likewise, staffulty discipline, posting and advertising for positions, and providing guidance and assistance when people need it most. Leaders do not need to be experts in human resources but should have a strong understanding of how the world of HR impacts those they lead.

- DELEGATION - This could easily be included in the section on time management. As leaders we tend to believe we can/should be doing it all. If we ask for others to do something, even a small task, we may feel we are showing that we are weak or incapable of doing the job. We must trust the people around us to do their jobs. Give them the skills, coach them, and let them go.

3. INSTRUCTIONAL LEADERSHIP: Most leaders were teachers prior to stepping into the role of school administrator. Serving a school as the instructional leader seems like an easy thing to do until the first time a new leader takes the reins. While most who take on the school leader role believe a great deal of their time will be spent in this area, research shows

the average principal spends less than 20% of their time on instruction related efforts. Nonetheless, guiding instructional programs, monitoring curriculum and learning environments, driving meaningful professional development, and evaluation of teachers can be all consuming and leave leaders feeling lost. Support in the area of instructional leadership may assist leaders in continually leading and living the mission and vision of their schools.

4. COMMUNICATION - Perhaps one of the most important and often missed skills of the leader is communication. Having all the knowledge but not sharing it does not help anyone grow or improve. Many leaders who get labeled as failing or struggling simply don't communicate well with others. This might be by oversight or by unintentional efforts. Some leaders don't hold staff meetings because they don't want to take away from their team's time. Valid point, but if you aren't giving them the information they would have gotten in that format you aren't being supportive. Most teachers will be happy to attend the meeting if the information is important, time is used wisely, and relevant outcomes are evident. Having a coach to support communication can show leaders where they miss opportunities to share with those who matter.

5. CLIMATE AND CULTURE - When we dive in and go to work it can be easy to miss impacts on the school culture and climate. Going through the course of a school year can wear on just about any person. Taking periodic steps to reinforce appreciation of staffulty and students is quite valuable. This might be dropping handwritten notes on everyone's desk, having a mac n' cheese cook-off on a professional development day, or handing out surprise ice cream bars at the end of the day to kids and staffulty. A coach can be that voice in your ear reminding you to keep the human beings at the forefront and not just standards, test scores, budgets, and the other things that quickly consume you as the leader. Remember...we are in the people business.

6. SPECIFIC FEEDBACK - At different times of a school year, as well as different points in our careers, feedback needs to be targeted at specific areas. Most of us can identify our strengths and our areas which need growth. One of the best things about having a coach is getting feedback on the things we're working to improve on.

YOUR BOSS AS YOUR COACH

Not everyone is going to have a coach provided as a district in-house support or as an outside consultant. So, can your boss be your coach? This is a great question and is really role specific. The superintendent who provided me with a coach had been neither a principal nor a teacher. The other superintendents for which I worked had been building principals, just not at the high school level. This allows those superintendents to support certain elements of my professional growth. For those they couldn't support, I relied on my network of other principals within the state.

When your boss has been in your role they can provide you coaching and support. One of my favorite parts of being a superintendent is helping my principals and assistant principals grow. I have great pride in them when I see their successes and moments of great leadership. As a principal, I took great pride in growing my assistants and those who I'd had as administrative interns. Being a coach for other leaders, along with their other responsibilities, can put a strain on their time. However, if the focus is really on growth, being intentional to set time aside on the calendar for the coaching cycle, or an abbreviated version, will allow for this work to happen. Being the boss and being the coach might best be summed up by Bradlee Skinner, a rockstar teacher and leader himself, and a former teacher of mine.

COACHING: DRIVER'S EDUCATION STYLE
BRADLEE W. SKINNER

At the start of my Sophomore year of high school I was able to begin the long standing rite of passage known as Driver's Education. As many new drivers experience, there is that thrill of operating a vehicle yet a feeling of trepidation at the same time in knowing what could happen if you mess things up. When I began learning with Darrin Peppard I had those very same feelings. I was excited to be teaching again and thrilled at the culture and climate of the school. It was truly unlike any educational environment I had ever experienced. However, a great deal of fear still existed within me as I was constantly worried that I might make a mistake. You see...I had some forward thinking ideas about education earlier in my teaching career which my educational leaders at the time were not too keen about. This led to criticism of my teaching, questioning of my skill, and doubting my ability to be an effective educator. As a result, I left education. When I returned to the classroom, with Darrin Peppard as my principal, I was still worried to try anything new or implement my ideas out of fear of being criticized or belittled.

When I first sat behind the wheel of the driver's ed. vehicle I knew I was ready, had the skills, and knowledge to do what I needed to do. I was confident yet weary. The instructor reassured me that all would be well. He showed me that even though I was in control of the car he had a brake pedal on his side of the car that he could operate to stop or slow things down if needed. This gave me the peace of mind I needed. That confidence I had was able to take full presence of my driving and the weariness I was feeling was taken up by the instructor as I knew he was there to help if things went wrong.

Darrin's leadership style was likened to my driver's ed. instructor. He did not do the driving or teaching for me (micromanaging) and he was not a backseat driver, constantly criticizing my performance. He let me implement my ideas without fear. He allowed me to take my classes where I knew they needed to be. And as I tend to do, in my eagerness to help students, I might be trying to do too much, too quickly. In those instances Darrin was there to tap that brake and slow things down to a manageable pace. Knowing that he was beside me but ultimately allowing me to drive and navigate my own journey gave me the confidence I needed to become the teacher I knew I could be.

LEVERAGING A PROFESSIONAL LEARNING NETWORK

I am amazed at the incredible access we have through a multitude of avenues to knowledge and to experts in our field. Every state in the union has an association for school leaders connected to the National Association of Secondary School Principals (NASSP) and National Association of Elementary School Principals (NAESP).

Being a member of my association in Wyoming as a principal gained me so many powerful relationships and connections, which really became a support network. As a leader, if you aren't connected or participating in these organizations you owe it to yourself to check it out.

Completing this manuscript during the COVID-19 global pandemic has shown even more so the power and compassion that permeates the education community worldwide. This is extremely evident on social media. The efforts to share what teachers and school leaders are doing to keep students engaged in learning has been exciting to see. This time in education will forever change what we do, and being connected to educators all over the world while learning a whole new way to practice our craft is inspiring. But it also reinforces why leaders need to be connected on social media.

Using these powerful tools puts me in contact with educators struggling with the same things I might be at any given time. My #1 is Twitter. This is great micro-PD at the tips of your fingers. Participating in a Twitter Chat, following a hashtag, or even sending direct messages to others has given me so many answers to questions I have had and, likewise that I've been able to answer for others. Want to learn about a cool new tool for engagement, productivity, or telling your school's story? You're going to find it on one, or all, of these platforms. In the appendix of this book, you'll find a list of must-follows on Twitter that I highly recommend.

BEING ACCOUNTABLE...TO YOU

In the end, your growth and success are in your hands. You are the person who looks back in the mirror each day. I am a believer in focusing on only that which we control. Too often I hear people complaining about things that happen to them or worrying about things they cannot control. Don't waste your time here. Whether you are able to have a coach to work with you or you simply start a cycle on your own, get out there on the balcony and take some stock. Get back to what you value and think deeply about your progress in those areas. It will make a difference. If you are willing to do that, then you are well on your way down the Road To Awesome!

CHAPTER NINE

ROAD TO AWESOME LEADERSHIP

> The road to success is always under construction.
> STEVE MARABOLI

Taking the leap from being a high school principal to becoming a superintendent filled me with both excitement and fear. I knew the new job would require some different skills and by changing states would also push my learning curve rather high. It also provided a unique opportunity for me that not every leader gets. I had the chance to reinvent myself as a leader when I became a superintendent. Not that I hadn't done things well as a high school principal, but taking this new role in a new location was a chance to refocus and reprioritize on how I wanted to lead and what my vision would be in this new district.

We have all heard the phrase, "If you fail to plan, you plan to fail." Taking on this new position brought this quote front and center for me. It caused me to realize how crucial this plan would be for my success and my district's success moving forward. Similarly, each school year brings for leaders the chance to reinvent or refocus their leadership efforts. The purpose of this chapter is just that, to refocus or allow you to reinvent your current leadership practices.

LOOKING BACK BEFORE GOING FORWARD

Throughout the course of this book I have focused on six big things that genuinely matter in leadership. The Game Changers if you will. The things you want on your dashboard, the critical elements to success in school leadership. Before you begin your planning, let's review the Game Changers. Below I have summarized each of the six game changers and provided some questions for your reflection. Think deeply about each of these questions, as they may be a part of your plan moving forward.

VISION - It is really difficult to hit a target you cannot see. Equally true is this statement for those you lead. Being clear about what you see on the horizon provides a road map for others to follow. People will rarely push back simply to be obstinate. This is usually the end result of unclear direction. Be upfront about what you expect. Make that expectation the standard by which all are measured and success is right around the bend.

- What do I value and what does my school stand for?

_____

_____

_____

- If someone asked my staff, students, and community what my school stands for, what would they say?

_____

_____

_____

_____

_____

_____

- Do the mission and vision statements reinforce what my school stands for? Why or why not?

_____

_____

_____

_____

- How do I make clear what my school stands for to all of my stakeholders?

_____

_____

_____

_____

CULTURE & CLIMATE - There may be nothing more important than the culture and climate of your school. At the same time, there may be nothing more overlooked. Leaders often focus on changing instructional practices, dive deep into data, or even tighten discipline, attendance, or dress codes in an attempt to improve student outcomes. While these steps have merit and may well provide some impact, without an intentional focus on culture and climate nothing done will reach its full potential. Culture and climate will change either way, it just may be that it gets worse as a result of no intentional work done in the area.

- 5 sentences that best summarize my school's culture would be:

_____

_____

_____

_____

_____

_____

- My school's mascot is the _____.

- Being a _____ means

_____.

- My school's brand is _____

_____.

- Engagement in my school, not just in the classroom but overall engagement/school spirit is best described as:

_____

_____

_____

STAFFULTY GROWTH & RECOGNITION - Teachers, paraprofessionals, custodians, secretaries, and everyone else who works with students (directly or indirectly) have similar needs. First, they all want to be included, to matter. Being intentional to recognize and thank those working day in and day out with kids is essential. Second, we all want to do our best work. Sometimes that means we need support, coaching, and feedback. Making a commitment to grow all staffulty builds a culture of importance and cohesiveness. This will also help reduce staffulty turnover.

- When I think about all the employees in my school, do I see a sense of unity or do clear divisions exist?

- Do I spend time in classrooms when kids are present? What about when they aren't? What are my current practices with meeting with staffulty?

- What am I currently doing to help grow and encourage my staff? How am I supporting their needs as professionals? As people?

_____

_____

_____

_____

_____

- What am I currently doing to recognize my staff? How do I build relationships and culture with my staff?

_____

_____

_____

_____

STUDENT VOICE & ACTION - Education today must put students in a position to make a difference in their communities. This might be through activities to support non-profit organizations, robust work-based learning, peer to peer leadership, or projects supporting their local area. It is said that our students are the future. Why do they have to wait? Allow students to use their voices and their actions to demonstrate their knowledge and learning now.

- Am I making a conscious effort to know my students by name? What do I know about my kids and their interests?

_____

_____

_____

_____

_____

_____

_____

- Am I making myself available to sit and talk with kids? Do they approach me with ideas? If so, how do I answer them?

_____

_____

_____

_____

- When I think about my most at-risk students, what message am I delivering (intentionally or unintentionally) to my students and my teachers? How am I working to support my most at-risk students?

_____

_____

_____

_____

BEING THE AUTHOR OF THE STORY - Each school has its own unique story. A story composed of both past and present accomplishments, struggles, successes, and traditions. In today's social media driven society, we have to be in control of the narrative. Finding the key methods to reach a variety of stakeholders with the stories of what is really happening inside the brick and mortar can be extremely impactful to the perception of the school within the community.

- What are the top 5 ways my school's story is being told? Who is leading that narrative?

_____

_____

_____

_____

- What forms of social media are in use at my school? What tools am I using to push information to parents, students, and community members?

_____

_____

- What type of communication is my school sending out? (List ten posts, emails, or other forms of sharing you or your school/district have shared. Now, categorize them as information, success stories, athletics, academics) Where is the bulk of my communication going?

_____

_____

_____

_____

_____

_____

_____

_____

_____

- What are the current perceptions held by the community of my school? What stories need to be told about my school to ensure the perception is accurate? What are three things I can do right now to share these stories?

_____

_____

_____

_____

_____

_____

_____

LEADERSHIP COACHING - Leadership is one of the few careers in which you are expected to be perfect on the first day and only get better as time passes. There is clear value in coaching. Even the best athletes in the world need coaches for feedback, guidance, and continued motivation. Coaching teachers is now an essential role for school leaders. But who is coaching the leaders? Ensuring leaders receive feedback and guidance might be one of the most important elements in leader success and retention.

• What am I currently focusing on as 'the work'? Do I feel it's the right work or do I need to reframe?

_____

_____

_____

_____

• Where is my 'balcony' space? Do I spend appropriate time there? Do I reflect on my practice and focus?

_____

_____

_____

_____

• Who is coaching me as a leader? Do I have someone who might provide an outside perspective to my work as a coach? Who might that person be?

_____

_____

_____

_____

You know when your principal, superintendent, curriculum director, or whoever calls the shots goes to a conference and comes back with the next BIG thing? You've barely even digested the last thing they asked of you and now it's time to make even more room on the ever shrinking plate. At one point in my career we had 13 different initiatives happening simultaneously. It was impossible to know when to do what. I was guilty of this as a leader too. I won't lie or pretend I didn't at one time add more without thinking. I'm asking you not to do that to your staffulty. You might have found something in this book that you want to implement right away. If so, and if it represents more on the plates of those you lead, then get back up on the balcony and see what you might be able to take away BEFORE you add to their already difficult jobs.

Instead, consider this plan. Put together a group and do a book study with Road To Awesome. Find a few things, or even just one thing, you and/or your team can do on your own. Remember that famous scene from City Slickers? Billy Crystal and Jack Palance discussing the secret of life. One Thing. And just like Palance's character Curly said to Billy Crystal's character Mitch when he asks what that one thing is, "It's up to you to figure that out." Find that one thing and CRUSH IT.

CONCLUSION

I have made clear what my priorities are, what I hold in high value, and how I choose to lead. But now it is your turn. This book would miss the mark if you didn't come away with a plan of action, a method by which you will become a better leader for your school, your district, your community. What I've outlined did not hit heavily on a focus on instruction, data analysis, or organizational management. I don't ignore those items by any stretch of the imagination. They are included in my day to day, week to week, and so forth. My plan hinges primarily on relationship building and reinforcing. Make no mistake about it, as leaders we still have to check all the boxes on our job description. However, we get to decide how we check those boxes and what we prioritize, how we piece it all together, and how we lead.

Leadership is messy. Leadership is not easy, and it is not for the faint of heart. Leadership is filled with challenging days — days when you might best be served with a good cry or guttural scream. But it's also filled with days of excitement, pride and thrill. Leadership is awesome! Leadership is game changing.

It's been nearly 25 years since Betsy first mentioned the leadership potential she saw in me. 25 years of learning. 25 years of growing.

Early in my career I was told to pay attention to everything other leaders do. I did. I learned from the mistakes I made. I learned from the mistakes of others. I learned that being a leader isn't just about being the front man, everyone deserves the spotlight. I learned to let go of what I couldn't control. If you can't control it, try not to lose sleep over it. I discovered that somebody else's opinion of me didn't matter. One day you may be their rockstar, the next you won't. Over time I began to realize that it was much less important to win an argument than it was to let someone know that they have been heard and understood. I learned to listen deeply. Speak last. You don't have to be the only person with an idea. I learned the importance of balance. Don't spend all your efforts on one item on the agenda. Trust those around you to do their part. Be supportive, give feedback, guide them, coach them, love them. And most of all, remember who you serve.

The Road to Awesome might not always be easy. If you work at it, learn and grow from it, you'll meet amazing people and do amazing things along the way. You'll hit a few potholes and you might even get lost. But that's the beauty of the learning journey.

When two roads diverged, I took the Road to Awesome.
Which road will you take?

ABOUT THE AUTHOR

D r. Darrin Peppard, a self-proclaimed recovering high school principal, a school district superintendent, speaker, author, and consultant. Darrin's expertise in school culture and climate, along with coaching and growing emerging leaders has made him a leading voice in school leadership on an international level.

Living life on the "Road To Awesome", Darrin leads through relationships, compassion, and a human-being first focus. He has served kids and adults as a superintendent, principal, assistant principal, teacher, and coach. Darrin was recognized as the Jostens Renaissance Educator of the Year in 2015, Wyoming Secondary School Principal of the Year by WASSP/

NASSP in 2016, and in 2019, he was inducted into the Jostens Renaissance Hall of Fame.

Darrin and his wife, Jessica, live in Grand County, Colorado spending as much time off the road in their Jeep and hiking with their daughter Liz and their dogs, Phoenix and Dexter.

The leadership journey is a road complete with twists and turns, bumps and straightaways, and times when it diverges in two. When the road diverges on your journey, take the Road to Awesome...and don't look back.

GET YOUR SCHOOL, EVENT, OR LEADERSHIP TEAM ON THE ROAD TO AWESOME WITH DARRIN

ROAD TO AWESOME: EMPOWER, LEAD, CHANGE THE GAME

We are in the people business, we can never forget this. This talk takes educators deep into their core beliefs, regardless of their role or level of experience, and inspires them to lead their classroom, school, or district down the Road to Awesome. Keynote for educational conferences, professional development, leadership team development.

GAME CHANGERS: 43 IDEAS FOR AWESOME SCHOOL CULTURE & CLIMATE

Building awesome school culture and climate takes intentional effort, time, and dedication. This fast-paced, idea-filled talk fires up attendees and leaves them with practical, easy to implement culture builders to get their classroom, school, or district on the Road to Awesome. Keynote or workshop for educational conference, professional development, leadership team development.

STUDENT DRIVEN SCHOOLS

The culture of our schools is not only driven by the adults but by the students. After all, they are who the schools are build for, right? This student focused session empowers students to think about their ability to lead, right now, in their school and community. Keynote, workshop, or student conference session.

COACHING & CONSULTING WITH DARRIN

Even the best athletes in the world need coaches for feedback, guidance, and continued motivation. Darrin will develop for you a customized plan supporting leaders of all experience levels and responsibilities. This work can be done in full leadership teams or with individuals. Contact Darrin for more information and a free consultation to see if this is the right investment for your school or district.

VISIT
ROADTOAWESOME.NET
TO GET CONNECTED
WITH DARRIN

CODE BREAKER LEADERSHIP SERIES

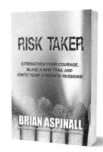

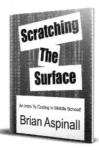

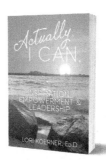

CODE BREAKER KID COLLECTION

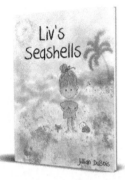

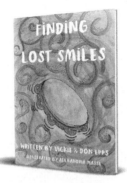

www.codebreakeredu.com